Most of us want to forget all the trauma we've endured. But as Connard Hogan so eloquently reminds us, life is not about the forgetting, it's about the remembering. In this brutally honest account, we are given a front row seat into the ghosts of one man's past, serving as a reflection of all that can be healed inside of us—as individuals, a nation, and as a world. Prepare yourself to plumb the depths of humanity and emerge with a grander perspective on the challenges that bring forth positive and lasting transformation.

—Cherie Kephart, award-winning author of
A Few Minor Adjustments

Very few who went to Vietnam left unscathed. It was physically traumatic, emotionally traumatic, or in many cases, both. *Barbwire, Brothels and Bombs in the Night: Surviving Vietnam* is the story of one young man's journey through the challenges of his military service in Vietnam. It is the chronicle of someone who, though he does not face combat, bears the psychic wounds of his coming of age in a wartime environment. Connard Hogan goes to Vietnam a naïve, inexperienced boy of twenty and returns no longer naïve and with experiences that are a far cry from what a boy becoming a man would normally encounter. From the extreme boredom of an office assignment, permeated with an ongoing fear of danger, to a warped sexual awakening in the arms of prostitutes, the year Connard spends in Vietnam, like for many vets, affects him for years to come. It is only when he recognizes the damage he has sustained that he has a chance, finally, to heal and move on.

—Dale Griffiths Stamos, author,
filmmaker and award-winning playwright

Barbwire, Brothels and Bombs in the Night: Surviving Vietnam offers provocative insight into the human frailties resulting from time spent in Vietnam during wartime. Connard quickly struggles with the amount of control held over him once he is drafted into service and repeatedly faces his mortality throughout his journey in Vietnam. I was surprised by the amount of toxic masculinity emerging from the pages and at times was disheartened by Connard's evident lack of respect for women. However, it is evident his involuntary military presence in a dangerous country far from home held a gloomy shroud over his psyche, nudging him into a world where vices may have meant survival. My husband was a medic in the Vietnam War, and he had his own demons. I am thankful Connard reached out for counseling and is now able to provide professional services to help others. His perspective on the war, while unique to me and difficult to comprehend, likely will be relatable to others who have been there and will provide some degree of understanding for those who have not.

—Martha Louise, author of
Married to Merlot: A Memoir with a Message of Hope

Connard Hogan's *Barbwire, Brothels and Bombs in the Night: Surviving Vietnam* proves that history repeats itself in this coming of age insider's view of repeated generational trauma from a traumatized Vietnam veteran who grew up in the shadow of his father's World War Two traumas, driving him toward a path in search of healing. There is a certain magic about the transformation that comes through healing and redemption which you will find here in *Barbwire, Brothels and Bombs in the Night: Surviving Vietnam.*

—Matthew J. Pallamary, author of
Spirit Matters and Holographicosmic Man

Camus once said we used to wonder where war lived and now we know, inside ourselves. Connard Hogan's book brings Camus' words to life as Connard, searching for the meaning of his life while fearful for his own mortality as a young man of twenty, takes the reader into his experience of war in Vietnam—a struggle that continued within his soul long after that war ended. There are many moments in these pages of perseverance and of healing that we can all recognize within ourselves and take solace from as we find our own way.

—Rebecca Robins, journalist and author of
The French Laundry: A Critical Study of the Relationship Of Ethics to Excellence in Restaurant Organization

A very engaging story—thoughtfully written and with plenty of emotional, physical tension and well-placed detail that made me connect and empathize with the author's plight and root for him to succeed.

—Amberly Finarelli, freelance editor

Barbwire, Brothels and Bombs in the Night: Surviving Vietnam by Connard Hogan marks an important and incisive addition to the literature and legacy of the war in Vietnam. In his searing (but ultimately inspiring) memoir, Hogan, who was drafted at age 20, mines his own experience as an Intelligence Analyst to shine a bright light on the dark currents of toxic masculinity, generational trauma, addiction and PTSD that combined to make the conflict in Vietnam America's most unpopular war, a war from which many never came home, and many more have yet to recover.

—Elizabeth Ridley, author, *Searching for Celia*

Barbwire, Brothels and Bombs in the Night

and

in the Night

SURVIVING VIETNAM

CONNARD HOGAN

AUTHORITY
PUBLISHING

BARBWIRE, BROTHELS AND BOMBS IN THE NIGHT
Surviving Vietnam
by Connard Hogan
1. HIS 027070 History/Wars; Conflicts/Vietnam War
2. BIO 008000 Biography; Autobiography/Military
3. BIO 026000 Biography; Autobiography/Personal Memoirs
ISBN: 979-8-88636-017-2 (paperback)
ISBN: 979-8-88636-018-9 (ebook)

Library of Congress Control Number: 2023904064

Cover design by Lewis Agrell

Printed in the United States of America

Authority Publishing
13389 Folsom Blvd #300-256
Folsom, CA 95630
800-877-1097
www.AuthorityPublishing.com

Dedication

For Ms. Edith Alpee,
my Western Kentucky University Counselor,
with deepest gratitude for listening without
judgment when I most needed to be heard

Table of Contents

Acknowledgments

I want to acknowledge those GIs who became my friends and allies, though we lost contact years ago. They contributed in ways, large and small, in helping me in my awkward and difficult transition into manhood during my military service and year in Vietnam.

I want to thank Pamela, a vital psychological anchor for me during that difficult period. (I hope life has treated her well.)

My gratitude goes to those who have guided me and offered constructive feedback on my writer's path: those in my critique groups, workshops, and writing classes.

A special thanks goes to Rebecca Robins, journalist/author, who went out of her way to provide me invaluable guidance regarding the early development of this memoir. She recognized a potential and provided guidance in the crafting of this story far beyond what I could've ever hoped.

Thanks to Dale Griffiths Stamos, author/filmmaker/playwright, who has been a writing instructor [mentor] to me and the editor on this manuscript. She helped shape it into a more compelling story.

My appreciation goes to Rachel Sarah Thurston, social media consultant at "State of Sparkle," who assisted me with developing my website, enhancing my social media platform, and strategizing book marketing.

Finally [last but certainly not least], thanks, appreciation, and love to my wife, Janet, who tolerates my idiosyncrasies daily.

May my words provide solace, inspiration, and encouragement to those who have struggled, are struggling, and are yet to struggle with trauma on their life's journey.

Walk in beauty.

Author's Note

This account is of my experiences in the US Army, including my one-year tour in Vietnam. I do not claim to speak for anyone other than myself. Mine is only one story of the 2,594,000 vets who served there, which includes the 58,000 plus who didn't return home alive.

Some names are fictitious, though all accounts are as accurate and true to my experiences as memory allows, and in no case did I intend to denigrate any individual.

Life within compounds surrounded by barbwire—the razor type—epitomized my life, though I escaped into the city of Nha Trang in pursuit of "recreation" during the first portion of my one-year tour. For me, barbwire symbolized the wall of illusion between safety and injury, though it morphed into a symbolic psychological barrier that I internalized. As such, I consider myself a silent casualty, left with the notion that emotional and spiritual scars from trauma are, in many cases, worse than physical wounds. Trauma does not remain silent. Its debilitating effects corrupt an individual's life until it is named and given a voice.

I wrote this story as a way to heal myself, in part, by acknowledging and remembering that which I experienced. I wrote it to provide a broader understanding of trauma to those who haven't experienced warfare, particularly those who underestimate 'Nam vet sacrifices. I wrote it for the loved ones of other vets, who—for whatever reason—didn't, can't, or won't share their experiences. In addition, I wrote it to offer a possible path forward for those suffering trauma, from whatever source or to whatever degree.

So, I sing my song, my story, the only way I know how, hoping others will hear it.

Hollywood production. Sure, I'd talked about 'Nam with friends in high school and around my neighborhood, but I'd never met anybody who'd been there, nor had I seen a protest in person. I lived in a backwater, I guessed, since weed hadn't made its way to anyone near me, either.

I hadn't studied Vietnam on the map … a deliberate dodge. Why did the "where" matter, anyway? Someplace in Southeast Asia, I knew, a colored shape on a classroom globe. May as well have been Peter Pan's Neverland for all I wanted to know.

Why Vietnam? To stop the spread of communism, was the pat answer, although I still hadn't determined what made that important. But I fully understood we'd been at odds with the Russians since the end of WWII over their acquisition of the atom bomb, the Berlin blockade, the Cuban missile crisis, and the space race.

How did a jungle or a rice paddy smell? I hadn't the slightest clue; there were none in Kentucky.

And what about those Viet Cong? From what I'd been led to believe, they were all brainwashed, uneducated rice-farmer peasants.

"I don't want to flunk out," I repeated. "I'd rather leave on my terms, not be ushered out by an academic bouncer." *Lose my school deferment for sure … likely … maybe not.*

"I wish I could change your mind. It's not too late."

I didn't stop to reconsider and saw no wiggle room, and though I had no idea what I'd do next, I was hell-bent on sticking to my decision. "No, I'm leaving," I said. "I've made up my mind." *How will Mom and Dad take the news?* I hadn't told them of my poor grades, nor my decision to quit. I didn't want to face the shame of my failure.

Dad had encouraged me to go to college and study engineering, unlike himself. He'd told me he left school after the fourth grade in order to work, but I never pushed him for the whole story. Besides,

FULL CIRCLE

"Trauma is personal. It does not disappear if it is not validated.
When it is ignored or invalidated the silent screams continue
internally heard only by the one held captive. When someone
enters the pain and hears the screams healing can begin."

—Danielle Bernock, *Emerging with Wings:*
A True Story of Lies, Pain, and the LOVE that Heals

My walk down the hallway and up the stairs of the psychology department building at Western Kentucky University carried me past the gauntlet of invisible ghosts from my past. *Can't be late. How much longer can I hold on?* My heart pounded in my ears. I avoided eye contact with people I passed along the way and hoped nobody recognized me.

I entered the counseling center office, not sure what to expect. Once inside, I informed a receptionist, "I have an appointment—"

"Take a seat," the girl behind the reception counter said with a smile. She picked up a phone and said in a cheery voice, "Your eleven o'clock is here."

What is she so happy about?

I checked my surroundings, noticing a few chairs, magazines on a table, brochures in a rack on the wall by the entrance, and bright overhead fluorescent lights. The doors to several interior offices were closed. I felt a gentle brush of cool air and heard piped-in music. The place smelled antiseptic. A typical reception area.

I couldn't concentrate on the music or the magazines. Couldn't concentrate on a single thing … other than my recycled thoughts of misery.

Several minutes passed before a plump, salt-and-pepper-haired woman appeared. She maintained a gentle gaze. "I'm Ms. Alpee," she said. "Let's go back to my office."

I followed her for a short walk to her inner sanctum.

She offered me a chair, then, seated behind her desk, asked me, "Why are you here?"

I took a deep breath. *I've got to start somewhere.* "I thought I could put Vietnam behind me, but I guess not. That and a girlfriend just dumped me. I can't handle it all."

At the age of twenty-three, I'd hoped to set aside the wreckage of my head-on collision with the realities I'd faced in Vietnam. Hoped I could lay those ghosts to rest, though now they were resurfacing, adding to the isolation and loneliness I experienced over the fresh loss of a girlfriend. At least, I'd considered her my girlfriend, though she didn't want to be mine at that point. I'd been plunged into turmoil. Everything churned, threatening to overwhelm and consume me, and ideas of suicide grew in frequency and intensity.

Now, as I look back on the crisis point that led me to that therapist's door, I can see more clearly how I had practiced a "slash and burn" mentality after my 'Nam tour and army service, trying to alleviate reminders. As a result, I'd lost contact with the buddies I'd had there almost immediately. Little did I realize at that time that I'd built walls, and topped them with barbwire, like those around the compounds where I'd lived and worked in Vietnam. Those walls kept others at a distance, and at the same time left me isolated and lonely. I've come to realize I hadn't appreciated the value of maintaining many of those relationships. I've wondered what kinds of emotional baggage those guys—and beyond that, everyone who served in 'Nam—dragged home, and what might've been for those we lost. Of the 2,594,000 who served there from early '65 until we withdrew in March '73, some 58,220 either didn't return alive or succumbed to their wounds afterward. More than 1,600 remain unaccounted for, perhaps become part of 'Nam jungle. Of all those we lost, 997 died their first day in-country and 1,448 died the day they were scheduled to leave.

I served as one of the twenty-two support personnel for every infantryman in the field, according to what I'd been told in AIT (Advanced Individual Training). And though I didn't experience direct combat, I've wondered how I returned to the States alive. Propelled by testosterone, how many unnecessary risks had I taken? If only a moment sooner or later? Here versus there? A right turn instead of a left? Regardless of my behavior while there, even when in my work office, bunk, or pursuit to get laid, I'd stewed in an ongoing dread of bodily harm and death, always forefront in my mind. As a result, forced to assess my safety frequently while struggling to define my manhood, I lived my particular brand of trauma. In addition, I grew disillusioned over my notions of what it meant to be American.

That war's impact on me lingers. My recurring bad dreams of duty re-activation after my discharge disappeared at some point, I'm glad to say, though I can't remember when. But part of my mind remains on alert, watching and listening. I grow anxious when I travel and prefer a window seat on a plane to observe the terrain. I maintain a beard; I'm stubborn that way. I carry my wallet in my front pocket to minimize the chance of its theft. Wanting to minimize living by a regimented schedule, I avoid wearing a watch. I store a field jacket in my garage. I wore it on occasion when hiking in earlier years, though rarely do so now. I wear a pair of my black stateside clodhoppers, scuffed raw at the toes, when I do heavy-duty work around the house and yard. Right after discharge, I gave one pair of my jungle boots to my brother. I abandoned the majority of my army-issued clothing to the care of my parents, and lost track of it. I kept my E-5 insignia rank pins, though have no idea when and where my dog tags disappeared.

In my mind, I proved my patriotism beyond doubt when I'd reported for draft induction, swore to defend the constitution, and wore an army uniform for more than two years and eight months. I gush with patriotism when I hear the anthem, and at times shed a tear. Sometimes I mouth a few words.

I won't place my hand over my heart nor salute. Nope. Been there, done that. I don't pledge allegiance to the flag anymore, either. Did that from my first day in school until I graduated high school … more than three thousand times, I figure. To whom do I need to prove anything further about my allegiance? I soured on the idea that those gestures reflect an individual's depth of patriotism. They now seem superficial, as I consider that my honorable discharge and service record document, DD-214, speak loudly enough for me.

I've examined our national Vietnam War Memorial in DC, and checked its mobile equivalent, "the Moving Wall." Found no names I recognized on either. But the name of one special guy I'd known should be there, somewhere. I can't recall his last name. His first name was Jeff, though I called him Jellybean. I still grieve Jellybean's loss, because in some way, he was me and I was him. I identified with him, saw him as gentle, willing to go along, eager to please, and innocent of the ways of an uncaring world.

I've often asked myself, Was my brand of the trauma of 'Nam permanently seared into my soul with a hot brand? Does anyone ever escape war without some form of trauma? For me, 'Nam became a confusing time of not only physical and emotional survival, but of growth, however awkward, across the threshold of childhood into manhood. And as more of my 'Nam memories have resurfaced over time, like a single file of infantry grunts returning from a deep jungle patrol—quiet, weary, unkempt, and dirtied, each one a member of the group but separate and unto himself—my recollections force me to accept that my 'Nam war never ended. And I realize that it's not about the forgetting ... it's about the remembering.

READY OR NOT

January 29, 1969, the day I'd dreaded since dropping out of engineering school. On that cold, overcast morning Dad parked our Chevy station wagon at the curb in front of the local draft board building in Louisville.

Mom, Dad, and I waited in silence for my scheduled rendezvous with transportation, and whatever would follow. We'd avoided mention of Vietnam to that point, or at least I did, as if some veil had descended. But I couldn't escape its constant reminders. Verlon, my younger brother by four and a half years, had stayed home to ready himself for school, and we'd exchanged our goodbyes there. Worry-wart Mom crushed the wadded tissue she used to wipe away her stream of tears. Dad remained still, facing straight ahead, reminded of his navy experiences in WWII, I guessed. Mom had told me he'd suffered nightmares after that war.

I unfolded and re-read my draft board papers for the umpteenth time. *No mistake. Report for induction into the US Army. ...* The slow asphalt roller of the draft process had caught up to me and made it clear that Uncle Sam wanted me. Reluctant to serve, I'd fantasized I'd be overlooked at the draft office, hoping some unseen power would wag a finger and push my records off a desk into a trash can, or a derelict alcoholic would drop a lit match and burn down the draft board building.

I wanted to avoid a Mom-meltdown, wanted to stay strong and say to her, "I'll be okay." Wanted to tell her not to worry. But I couldn't. Doubts swirled about the decisions that had led to my current circumstance, and dread mixed with sadness over departing from the two people always nearby. I was about to go into the future where new possibilities would lead me into manhood ... or a body bag.

* * *

Ten months earlier, my heart had pounded as I faced the school dean behind his desk. "I've decided to quit," I'd told him with a dry mouth. I couldn't face flunking out.

From high school I'd enrolled in the University of Louisville's Speed Scientific School (I'd planned for an engineering degree since junior high), but that was not to evade the draft. War just wasn't part of my equation. In high school, I hadn't studied much—hadn't needed to—but college engineering classes increased in difficulty, and poor grades led me to probationary status by the end of my freshman year.

"Why?" the dean asked.

He was in his fifties, I guessed. His loosened dark-red tie stood out against a white shirt, sleeves rolled up. A tweed sports coat draped across the back of his swivel chair. A cowlick stuck out from the back of his head, highlighting his male-pattern baldness.

"This is my third quarter on academic probation and I don't want to flunk out."

His forehead wrinkled. "Don't you know you'll end up in Vietnam?"

Vietnam? A situation to avoid, but I'll cross that bridge.... .

Vietnam on TV didn't seem real—too easy to dismiss the whole uproar as an issue for somebody else, or downplay as just another

I'd heard him stretch the truth on occasion. I wasn't sure about his WWII stories, but had no other reason to doubt what he said.

As I left the dean's office, I rehashed questions that had plagued me the last several months. Were my bad grades a result of my lax study habits? Or because I couldn't cut the mustard, no matter what, even though I'd attended all the classes and completed the assignments and lab work? But no clear answer was evident, and a nagging suspicion lurked that my dropping out stemmed from something much deeper. No matter, I wanted to make my own decisions and avoid talking with Mom and Dad about them.

Faculty had forewarned all of us freshman students about attrition. Those of us who'd returned each successive quarter noted smaller class sizes and talked of those who'd disappeared. So-and-so dropped out. So-and-so couldn't make the grade. Now I'd be one of those who'd gone missing.

It didn't take long for me to enroll in the technical school at the college, figuring the evening courses would provide me cover from the draft board and so I settled in. I studied electrical circuitry along with navy nuke submariners. I couldn't avoid their constant talk about submarine duty. Not that the information about nuke subs didn't interest me, but everything boiled down to the fact that I couldn't square myself with their military-lifer ideas. Couldn't relate. But my draft notice, when it arrived, proved my tech-school plan was like a screen door on a submarine: full of holes.

I hadn't explored other draft evasion maneuvers. Enroll in a different college? I had no idea what I wanted to study at that point. The "where" didn't enter the picture. Money had been a big obstacle, so I'd remained at home to cut down on expenses. Marry? I didn't even have a girlfriend, much less know someone who'd consider that sham arrangement to skirt the law. Get a medical deferment? I suffered no medical issues that required a visit to a doctor. I did keep a card up my sleeve, though an imperfect one. Canada as an escape option cropped up as often as war casualty reports, but that didn't fit my notion of a good plan—uprooting to a strange land with no friends, no job, no money—and what would everyone who knew me think about that anyway?

* * *

As Mom, Dad, and I sat, I rehearsed how to begin my goodbye and hoped Mom would start first. My jumbled thoughts crowded together in a wad. Unable to rid myself of the mental hairball, I worked to maintain my sense of dignity and not run away like a screaming lunatic.

A school bus pulled up, painted a drab army color like olive-green or light-brown. Who cared?

After a deep breath, I said, "I guess I'd better go." I leaned over the front seat to hug her, and said, "Bye, Mom."

Surprised by my sudden move, Mom gushed tears.

A last-second verbal cram session began. Our words crowded together.

"I love you, sweetie." She held tight as I started to pull away.

I wanted to say, Don't cling, but instead echoed, "I love you, too." I responded to her pleas with "Okay, Mom, I'll be careful." *Always be there for me ... when I need you.* Of course, I couldn't say that either, fearful I'd cry, too. "Yeah, I'll call when I can and come home as soon as I get a pass."

We expected I'd call them from Basic, and come home for a visit. Fort Knox lay fifty-some miles down the road, not far from Gramma's and Grampa's farm in Upton.

I turned to hug Dad. "Bye, Dad."

He hesitated. "Bye, son."

I didn't want to leave, but saw no other choice—a last-minute fast break to Canada ruled out—and I didn't want to look like a sissy in front of the other males converging on the bus. A quick departure seemed easiest. I said, "No need to get out into the cold. You guys stay in the car."

Out and away from our Chevy wagon, I felt like a scab had been ripped off my soul. I took a last look after a few steps, waved, and said, "Bye."

Then I turned my head toward my future.

* * *

Fear had often gripped me as a kid, compelled me to avoid Dad's wild green-eyed stare when it was accompanied by alcohol-angry breath, but I learned that when his eyes were soft, he joked, told interesting stories, and had a warm, beating heart. I loved those green eyes in spite of my fear and had adopted strategies of evasion and defense against Dad.

Like the time he'd mispronounced my name.

In the middle of a school week, I'd completed my homework before supper, so after we'd eaten, Mom told me I could watch TV.

I lay stretched on the couch, belly down, propped up on my elbows, minding my business when Dad arrived home and came straight to me.

"Con*ard*," he said, using an "ard" sound as in aardvark, rather than the usual way he and Mom had always pronounced it with an "erd" sound, as in shepherd.

"Don't," I said, "I'm watching TV."

"Con*ard*, Con*ard*, Con*ard*," he repeated.

"Stop. Why are you doing this?" When I looked at him, I noticed his fixed stare and strange grin. *Been drinking?*

"Con*ard*, Con*ard*, Con*ard*," he repeated.

"Dooon't," I said, "you're making me want to cry."

He continued his taunt, "Con*ard*, Con*ard*, Con*ard*."

"Stoooop. Why are you being mean?" I figured he loved me, pretty sure. But this left me puzzled.

After he relented, I decided I wouldn't let him do that to me again.

The next morning, my fourth-grade teacher called me to her desk in front of the class. "You've misspelled your name," she said, loud enough that everyone heard.

As her accusing finger pointed at my homework, I gave her my truth. "No, I didn't."

She repeated herself and tapped the paper with her finger where I'd written my name.

I'd come that far; I didn't waver an inch and said, "No, I didn't." I wondered if she'd make me go to the principal's office, but she said nothing else. I didn't tell her I'd changed the spelling the night before because of Dad.

* * *

A new kind of fear gripped me as I walked through the chilled air and away from Mom and Dad ... different, bigger, impersonal, and beyond my sight and touch. Could it, would it swallow me whole and not leave a trace? I'd become an anonymous number, my fate determined by others I'd never meet. I couldn't appreciate that one iota.

I clambered onto the bus. The rubber aisle mat muffled the footsteps of young guys ahead and behind me. Midway down the aisle, I slid into an empty seat. Closed windows with corners of condensation intensified the mixed odors of rubber, fake leather, and who knew what else. Indifferent. Unwelcoming.

With one hand I wiped a swath of water from my window and watched the passing scenery along the way to army induction, wherever that would be. I envied pedestrians and drivers going about humdrum activities, and figured most never gave the bus on which I rode a first glance, or if they did, a second thought.

Nobody on that bus had volunteered to be there, I'd have bet. You'd find no hitchhikers on board. Everyone remained quiet like we were headed to a funeral.

* * *

Halfway down the line where I stood, stripped to socks and briefs as instructed, with shirt and pants draped over one arm and shoes in hand, I'd advanced to the final induction-physical station. The doc stayed on point, didn't chitchat. "Got any problems we need to know about?" he asked me after he'd fingered my private parts, checking for a hernia.

I crossed my fingers and pointed. "Just this." My sock stuck to my red and oozing big toe from crusted pus. *Will an in-grown toenail save my bacon with a medical deferment?*

"Let me take a look," he said.

I pulled off my sock.

"Not a big deal," he said, without even a flinch or a blink. "They'll take care of that later. You're good to go. Get your clothes on."

Damn. Taken, and not with a bang but a whimper.

Once the doc completed his exam of everyone in my group, a guy dressed in fatigues and younger than me took over. "Take a seat in the waiting room and remain quiet," he demanded.

Those cleared for induction arrived a dozen at a time. When the room filled, the same guy said, "Listen up," and gestured with one hand. "Head into that room and form up in lines."

* * *

It was hard to miss the Stars and Stripes against dark-brown wood-grain paneling and the light reflected off the framed mug shot of Richard Nixon nearby.

A captain took up position next to the flag and faced the cluster of males packed into the room, all dressed in civvies and barely able to grow whiskers. The captain began, "You need to swear an oath of allegiance to defend the Constitution of the United States. Raise your right hand and repeat after me."

"I," we started, then I said my name aloud, "do solemnly swear... ." My voice joined the chorus of a motley crew of strangers, equally entering the commitment to the vast, sprawling collective, each on an individual path to his destiny.

"Now, you're in the army," the captain said.

I'm fucked. A little cog in a huge machine. When will I be free again?

* * *

Third day in, Sergeant Stone, crisp, mid-twenties, bellowed, "Form up, recruits, you're going to give blood."

I don't want to give blood.

We marched a short distance, then a different instructor segregated the formation. "Anyone ever convicted of a felony? Raise your hand."

Criminal types, separated from us with the wave of a hand and then ordered, "Form up over there, maggots," gathered into a distinct package of little sausages.

Somewhere behind me, Stone marched them off.

The instructor took up position front-and-center of the thinned formation. "You have an opportunity to take aptitude tests to determine your MOS."

A standard line, repeated many times before, no doubt.

"For you ladies who don't know, MOS stands for military occupational specialty, a job description. It determines what you'll do in the army." He took one step to the side. "Recruit," the instructor said, focusing on one individual, "wipe that smirk off your face."

Subdued chuckles erupted from the formation.

"No snickering," he yelled. "Don't you dare snicker! Shape up or I'll kick your asses." He stared with the intent to melt hardened steel.

Me, inducted into the army as a two-year draftee, damn near shanghaied, I stood muted and at his mercy.

No doubt the army considered me an unruly, snot-nosed kindergartner—sit still, don't fidget, raise your hand before you talk, stay in line, hold hands when crossing the street, tell the teacher when you need to pee—except army in-processing was thrown in our faces, kick-ass, no sympathy and twenty-four-seven. Growing up, I'd enjoyed considerable latitude about what I did and how I did it. Mom was light-handed and tolerant with me and I learned how to minimize Dad's interventions. The army was going to take a lot of adjustment.

Somebody mumbled, words squeezed from a clenched jaw, "Don't cooperate with them."

From the corner of my eye I saw the instructor pace to one end of the formation, then study us. "If you don't want to take the aptitude tests, you'll join the others to give blood."

Choice? The army's providing me a choice? Suspicion spread through my thoughts like germs in elementary school. Spoken by a mere mortal, I would've understood, but this was from someone I considered my master at that moment: Lord of the Maggots.

"If you're willing to enlist for three years, you'll be guaranteed that MOS."

What the hell is he saying? I don't want to spend the rest of my life in the army.

"Most of you, guaranteed, will end up in 'Nam in the infantry."

What? The unmentionable confirmed, what I'd feared all along: 'Nam in the infantry—a death warrant.

The water had been brought to a boil, the coup de grace delivered as good as from the mouth of God. The formation stood silent. He moved into my direct line of vision and pursed his lips. "But … no pressure, mind you. Your choice."

I'd volunteer for a bit part in *The Green Berets*, but this guy wasn't talking about some Hollywood acting gig.

To enlist or not to enlist, that was the question. *If I wanted blood and guts, I'd have joined the marines, Oorah.* I swallowed hard … and chose the test.

* * *

Two days after I'd taken the test, they marched a bunch of us over to the test building. I scanned the posted list. Right there in black and white, next to my name: 96B20.

Yeah. Maybe, no lie, no sick joke. Maybe … I could be an "Intelligence Analyst"—whatever that is—instead of an infantryman. Maybe … I could avoid getting my ass shot off in 'Nam.

An instructor prompted me to take a seat at a table. He pointed a finger to an X on papers that had been typed in triplicate. "You're qualified to become an Intelligence Analyst, Ninety-Six Bravo Twenty," he said.

That's good, right?

"Just sign here," he went on. "You can use my pen."

How nice of you. I picked up his pen. I didn't want to spend any additional time in the army, but my butt was at stake.

It only took me two seconds to give over the next three years of my life by signing on that dotted line, as so indicated.

What have I done?

INTO THE WILD BLUE

Five months after my army induction, I'd expected delivery to 'Nam on military transport, painted drab olive-green, puke-beige, or a camouflage pattern—not the shiny commercial jet with bright red-and-white markings that I was now preparing to board.

A stewardess with a big smile stood inside the plane opposite the doorway.

Where were you during my thirty-day leave?

Headed down the aisle, I spied two more at the back of the plane in the galley.

Oh là là.

"Proceed to the last empty row and take the seat closest to the window on both sides. Occupy every seat until that row is filled," the army captain ordered. "Keep your hands to yourselves." Several other non-com lifers repeated the same monologue as the line of reluctant travelers entered the plane and moved down the aisle.

Every seat was filled. "Keep your hands to yourselves," the noncoms barked again.

They knew what this bunch of testosterone-filled males was thinking. What males wouldn't have in our situation? I wouldn't have dared play grab-ass regardless, though those thoughts and more crossed my mind. But I expected some of those other guys could be pretty bold.

"What are they going to do, send me to 'Nam?" somebody mumbled.

We lifted off and climbed out of Travis Air Force Base.

Friendly, dressed in their dark-blue two-piece uniforms, the stewardesses smiled and went about their work professionally. I watched them every chance I got, though worked to avoid being seen with my tongue hanging out. They seduced me with every move, regardless of their intention.

On her rounds, one stewardess asked me, "Would you like some water or a Coke?"

"Coke, please," I said, then caught a whiff of flowery perfume, or maybe shampoo—didn't matter to me which—as I accepted the glass from her delicate hand.

I watched her until my view got blocked. Nearly drew blood from biting my lip. *Worse than going to 'Nam, I'll arrive there a virgin. Pathetic, Connard, truly pathetic.*

Since my early teens, desperate and engulfed in the persistent drumbeat of male hormones, I'd wanted a girl to scratch my sexual itch, but fate had led me down a tortured path and filled me to the bursting point.

Primed by the fact that a female goat would hold sex appeal for me (in the right light), a stewardess' soft breast brushed against me or a touch of bare flesh, or even the faintest hint of the musk from an armpit challenged me with the invitation to respond with that primal male reaction. At least I could adjust myself and put the tray table down to conceal my recurring stiffy.

The stewardesses, no doubt trained in appropriate countermeasures and evasive action, understood that the young crowd around them, steeped in testosterone up to our eyeballs, could spring a leak.

I couldn't help but wonder what those gorgeous ladies were thinking and feeling. Scared of us or for us? Sad or helpless about our plight? Did they pity us? But as they looked into the faces around them and provided the last vestige of feminine kindness, they had to know body bags awaited the return to the States for an unknown number of us.

No amount of their kindness helped me overcome my sense of doom. On the contrary, their behavior served as a tease, accentuating what I'd left behind and what I'd be missing.

Our TV 'Nam jungle-war had entered my life in sound bites and clever camera shots. Upon our arrival, I'd become a bit player in the unfolding drama, on the front side of the camera, with a single-minded purpose: survival. I would've bet that everyone on board, even the flight crew, had the same thought.

Casual chat hid my quiet panic. I wanted to make believe the flight was no big deal by asking questions of my seat row companions. What's your MOS, and, Where're you from? Didn't work.

The guy next to me going home without an arm or leg? Shouldn't get personal, I'll likely never see him again. Not the time or place to make friends. 'Nam ... huh, not summer camp.

Drawn by the loud voices of several guys across the aisle, I focused on the one in the closest seat. *Loudmouth. Return home in a body bag?*

The guy in front of me reclined his seat and cramped my space. *Will he live through next week?*

The silence between our words spoke everything. Pensive, we sat, mostly a hushed gathering at a wake, though no one knew for whose death.

A mindless string of seconds became minutes, which turned to hours.

Unable to relax, I wallowed in the god-awful, nauseating dread in the pit of my soul. I thought about my wasted opportunities, what I'd done ... what I hadn't. My life, marked by a two-part question that occupied the top of the heap of smaller ones: Would I die ... and as a virgin?

* * *

We stopped for a layover in Honolulu, with enough time to explore the terminal.

Propped against a railing on an outside upper deck of the terminal, a warm breeze tugged on the hairs of my bare arms as dark-green palm fronds swayed. All around me moved tanned, smiling women with flowing hair and tantalizing breasts that invited caresses and exploration. Hawaii teased me and thumbed its nose, within my reach but off-limits. Hawaii's promises remained in the future, a long way off if I survived 'Nam, and at twenty that seemed an eternity away. A full-throated yell threatened to burst through my thin veneer of calm.

* * *

Our plane stopped to refuel in Guam.

Subdued like chaperoned prison inmates allowed into the yard for exercise, we filed into the terminal. The heavy air, musty and molded, suggested something ancient and unchanged. The heat, along with the humidity, stifled me—quite unlike the pleasant air of California—and hinted at what lay ahead.

Already, my memories of that and those left behind shifted. The bad dropped away and left the good, a scaffold onto which I began to construct a utopia. Each of my memories suddenly significant, they took on special qualities. Memories of my country, a place where we strive for a perfect and fulfilled life. Memories of home, family and friends, my Ford Fairlane, and favorite hangouts in the search to explore young femaleness.

Though my surroundings were foreign, I felt a deeper connection to Dad. I'd honed in on his WWII stories with horse ears, and he'd mentioned being in Guam.

"They went down the line at navy induction, and every third man went to the marines," he'd said, straight-faced. "I ended up in the navy and couldn't swim." A broad smile came over his face, then he chuckled. "They threw me into the water during basic training. Well, that didn't help; I damn near drowned."

I'd gobbled the informational crumbs he rationed over the years. Listened in awe and when I pressed for more, he'd give a short answer and soon change the subject. I figured he'd tell me more if and when he wanted, and that nobody could drag it out of him otherwise. I filled in the blanks with what I saw in war movies and the yellowed, framed photo of a ship that he kept on the wall.

I'd puzzled over the picture of that odd thing with its front doors open, beached on the sand near palm trees. When I'd asked, he explained, "I was assigned to that ship, an LST (Landing Ship, Tank). We carried marines, tanks, trucks, and jeeps. A few months after that picture I ended up in the water when it was sunk in action."

I'd wondered how he'd survived. He'd never learned to swim. But I hadn't pressed him on that point, figuring he didn't want to reveal those details.

I recalled the time he'd said, "I drove a landing craft to and from the beaches on Peleliu, one of the bloodiest battles in the Pacific." I thought I'd detected a break in his voice when he went on, "Something nobody should ever have to see."

I'd wanted to cry. Hadn't.

As we remained seated in the terminal, a hard rain fell.

What waited for me?

I replayed the goodbye scenes at home when I'd prepared for San Francisco, and beyond, at the end of my thirty-day leave after Basic and Advanced Individual Training.

Mom had sobbed off and on during my leave. Dad and my brother Verlon remained quiet.

Best case, I'd be gone a year. I tried not to think about the worst case. My attempts to reassure Mom about 'Nam were futile. I hadn't been able to reassure her of anything … not anyone, not even myself. Dad, Verlon, and I didn't touch the subject, though I would've bet it churned in their minds, too.

I managed a good face, that's all, with the picture of the other end of my year in 'Nam clouded by too many possibilities.

Bags packed and in khaki uniform, I'd stalled as long as I could, dreading saying the words, "I guess it's time to go." Roger, my friend and neighbor, waited for me at his house across the street.

Mom pleaded, "Write often," and begged, "Be careful." Her body spasmed as we hugged.

"I will, Mom," I replied. Lost for what else to say, I added, "Don't worry."

"I love you," she said for the umpteenth time.

"I know, me too," I said, awkward in the face of her repetitions.

With a quick hug and a slap on the back, Dad's goodbye was short and sweet. "Take care, son."

"Okay, Dad." I'd hoped for more than a meager sentence from him … but no way I could say that to him.

"Hey, bro, take care of yourself," Verlon said and offered a hug, too.

We slapped each other on the back.

"Yeah, you too," I replied and, as promised, handed him the keys to my '57 Ford Fairlane. "Here you go." *A bequeath?* "Hate to tell you, but I stripped second gear a couple of days ago."

His enthusiasm drained away.

"Sorry, bro," I added. Didn't mention I'd stripped that gear in an angry fit. Didn't mention I feared he might have an angry fit, too, and kill himself in a car wreck. "Watch out for the draft." I couldn't think of a single thing to add. What else had there been to say?

When Roger answered his front door, I said, "Ready? We'd better get going."

His mom gave him a last-second round of, "Goodbye," and, "I love you," as well.

Roger's dad drove us to the airport, where we caught our plane to St. Louis on our way to Vietnam in-processing on Treasure Island in the San Francisco Bay. As it turned out, the army also ordered Roger, drafted one day before me, to 'Nam—one day ahead of me.

I wanted to experience San Francisco and free love with hippie females, so I figured leaving home one day earlier didn't make a big difference. Another day wouldn't have reduced the heartache of my departure one smidgen. Besides, I'd known the last face-to-face goodbye would prove the most difficult, anyway.

*　*　*

After what seemed a moment's rest, all too brief, we re-boarded the plane, en route to our collective futures.

At mealtime, a stewardess stopped and asked me, "Would you like a glass of water or a Coke with your meal?"

I wallowed in her soothing voice and the way her lips parted as she spoke, the softness in her eyes, the way her hair hung as she leaned toward me, and her faint, sweet fragrance. "Coke, please."

As she moved away, I focused on her curves. *Delicious.* But her voice had sounded familiar somehow.

Dim at first, an image emerged. I pictured myself at seven years old and on our family couch in front of the TV, and hearing Mom's voice coming from the kitchen. Then I realized, That's why the stewardess' voice sounded familiar! *Jesus, how warped is my head?* I hadn't wanted to think of that stewardess in terms of my mother, but she, like my mother, exhibited the same qualities of tenderness and caring, toward which I felt pulled.

Other memories flooded in. Images from TV about a land where the good guy wore a white hat, vanquished the evils of the world, and punished the bad guy, while my brother and I made silly jokes, farted, and giggled in the warm security blanket of Mom's presence. Hollywood movie images of American soldiers flashed through my mind. The wounded who'd cried out at the sight of their blood as death closed in upon them. Cried out to return to places and times of comforting safety. Cried out for their mothers and pleaded with every ounce of energy ... to be there, once again ... watching their version of *Howdy Doody* on Saturday mornings with milk and cookies.

If only I can survive the coming year... .

WELCOME TO 'NAM

"We're beginning our descent into Tan Son Nhut," the pilot announced.

Whooooosh! A rush of warm, humid air circulated through the cabin, carrying the smell of corrupted vegetation, a jungle of living and dying—thick, heavy, and hidden in darkness. I felt a sense of suffocation. Constrained by my circumstances, and forced to remain buckled to my seat while being propelled into my unknown future, my lungs threatened to seize. My throat threatened to slam shut. Every cell of my body wanted to deny reality.

Before the plane rolled to a stop, a sergeant started, "If we encounter incoming rounds, keep moving until you're off the plane, and get to a bunker or hit the deck." His instructions, straightforward, amounted to a no-bones-about-it slap in the face. As if those words weren't enough, he delivered another swift kick in the ass. "The plane's engines will continue running. Once we're off and an outgoing group boards, this plane will leave."

That comment extinguished the last possibility of my escaping 'Nam. Reality had come home to roost. *You ain't in Kansas, anymore, Dorothy.* However unrealistic my hopes had been, there was no way around the fact that I'd arrived in 'Nam … and wasn't leaving anytime soon. And it wasn't like I thought I'd hide in the plane's lavatory or cargo hold.

Dirt had been thrown into my gaping wound. Fear welled up. The same unspoken fear I'd faced as a kid when I played hide-and-seek. Hidden, I'd wondered: if the others gave up the game, would they tell me? I could be left waiting for who knew how long. And those times, when on the verge of bursting, I'd emerge and run for home.

Suck it up, soldier. I had no idea what that would mean, however.

Meager solace, I'd not be left alone in 'Nam, though Nixon had started our "drawdown" from 543,000 men and women. And although individual members left daily and others arrived to replace them, that remained of little consequence to me. I was in 'Nam to stay until the army said otherwise.

Nonetheless, I felt like a participant in an adult version of hide-and-seek in 'Nam: me on the American-allied team, lined up against the VC and NVA. But there wouldn't be the giggled relief when one team tagged the other and the game could start over, with everybody getting another chance and the worst consequence equating to a wedgie. No! 'Nam was played for keeps, and at twenty, though my death would be a personal tragedy, dying a virgin struck me as a sacrilege.

Tensed, my muscles readied me to move ... somewhere, anywhere. My gut knotted and a flush of perspiration covered my face. Stifling, jungle smells hung heavy in the airplane cabin and remained foreign and unsettling.

I surveyed the stewardesses' faces, wondering what lay behind their smiles. I tried to imagine their flesh against mine. Inhaling deep, I grabbed for any feminine scent I could take with me before I turned my head toward 'Nam, beyond the exit.

I expected a mortar attack any second.

CAMP SHIT-BURN

Pronto, I was off the plane, onto a bus, gone from the airfield, and delivered to the Long Binh In-processing Center.

The bus driver brought us to a stop. "Grab your duffles and dismount. Enjoy your stay."

No time for jokes. I could be dead in a minute.

A wet-dog smell, along with a cloud of dust carried by a gust of wind, greeted me when I stepped off the bus. *Will I melt in the heat and humidity?*

A sergeant standing nearby pointed an index finger toward a building. "You're assigned to that barrack. Go in and plant your ass on an empty bunk."

Yeah, yeah.

Another no-frills army accommodation greeted me, the same forest-green linoleum flooring, wood-beam support columns, bunk beds in rows, spaced six feet apart, the same as at Basic and Advanced Individual Training. What was new was the odor of 'Nam rot, and the where-am-I-and-how-did-I get-here questions that clogged my head. When would a half-crazed sergeant burst in, screaming orders and berating me?

One naked pillow and folded wool blanket rested on a thin mattress on each of the standard-issue metal-frame bunks. I tested one at floor level. *Saggy. Nothing new.* I lifted the mattress on one side and adjusted the wooden slats underneath. *Useless effort.*

I recognized the sergeant when he entered from the rear door. "I'm in charge of you here until you leave for your unit assignment. Remember your barrack number. Latrines … ." He pointed. "For the mess hall go out the front door, turn to your left. Communal showers … ."

Blah, blah.

He'd continued without pause, "You're expected to stay here except when on detail, at mess or in the latrine or shower. I'll see you every day."

Standard speech, no doubt.

"Don't wander off."

Wouldn't dare.

"Safeguard your gear and personal items from theft at all times. Any questions?"

Theft?

"How do we safeguard our gear when we shower or take a crap?" the guy next to me asked.

"Keep your valuables on you or out of sight, or try a buddy system," the sergeant said. "Any other questions?"

None, not a single word.

"Good. Form a line here. When I've verified your name, grab a clean set of bedding from the pile." He gestured toward a stack of folded sheets and pillowcases. "Keep your bunks properly made after reveille." One by one, he placed a check by each name on a prepared list, until he ticked off the last man's name. "Okay, I'm done. Make those bunks."

* * *

The guy in the bunk next to me stood up and said to me, "Hey, will you watch my stuff? I need to take a dump."

"Yeah. I got no place else to go at the moment." Wished I did.

My temporary neighbor, returned from his trip to the latrine, reclined on his bunk.

"My turn to hit the shitter," I told him.

A line of a half-dozen wooden latrines stood sentinel, each one designed for a single occupant at a time. Raised off the ground about four feet, they were constructed of wood planks. Simple and not difficult to build, they weren't your five-star accommodations. They reminded me of the outhouse at my grandparents' farm. Forty feet beyond them, strands of coiled concertina wire formed a soft perimeter around the in-processing center. I didn't give the wire a second look. I focused on the knee-high grass beyond the perimeter for any individuals dressed in black pajamas. Then I singled out a latrine whose door was open, and climbed the four wooden steps.

"Jesus!" I waved my hand. Didn't help. My grandparents' Kentucky outhouse never got that ripe. An urge to puke stifled, I locked the door from the inside, then opened my mouth for a breath. Would've sworn I could taste shit. I tried not to breathe. That didn't work! *Welcome to 'Nam, Dorothy.*

* * *

Each day brought involuntary assignments to a work detail for the ever-rotating supply of FNGs, Fucking New Guys, getting their initiation to 'Nam-style army chores.

Separated from the herd for work detail, five FNGs, me included, lounged on bags of dirty laundry while we waited for further instructions.

A sergeant appeared. "I need you to clean two rooms," he announced. I'd never seen him before. "Which one of you holds the highest rank?"

No clue, we looked around at one another's faces and rank insignias for an answer.

My previous volunteer experiences had been positive, as far as I'd determined, so I raised my hand. Maybe I'd earned a little respect with my E-4 rank.

As an inductee into the army, I'd started as an E-0, then promoted to E-1 private during basic training. Somewhere between there and my completion of AIT (Advanced Individual Training), I'd been promoted to E-4—the equivalent of corporal, though I was referred to as a Specialist. Big whoop. I hadn't done anything outstanding to get promoted; everyone around me who'd kept their finger out of their nose or ass had gotten promoted.

He noted my name tag sewn to my fatigue blouse. "Hogan. Okay, all of you follow me."

Led to a nearby barrack, he showed me the first and second floors, both empty. No bunks, no furniture, only the familiar dark-green linoleum flooring.

"Remove any trash and sweep and mop the floors," he said.

Busy work, if you ask me.

He pointed to a collection of trash bags, brooms, and mops in buckets gathered together in one corner on the first floor. "You'll need those tools. Any questions?"

Conversation will only complicate my situation. "No," I said.

"Good. Report back to me when you're done." He turned heel and marched off.

Wonderful. Responsible for cleaning empty fucking rooms.

Tasks sorted and delegated, I shuffled between the first and second floors to oversee the work.

The downstairs cleaned, I dismissed those two guys and headed back up to survey that situation.

How difficult is it for two guys to sweep and mop an empty room? "Come on, guys, this isn't hard." I grabbed a broom to speed things along.

A small, enclosed space occupied one corner of the larger room.

I told one guy, "Would you mop that corner room? Let me know when you're finished and you can go." I considered that a brilliant ploy. My way to encourage cooperation and gain quick completion of a mission that some officer, somewhere, considered important.

I mopped the floor of the larger room alongside the other fellow.

A few minutes passed. I heard nothing from the corner room.

With a quick check, I discovered the guy assigned to the corner room gone and fresh yellow piss pooled in one corner. "Fucking slob!" I yelled.

The other FNG hurried over.

"Hey, what's that guy's name?" I asked. Hadn't thought I'd need to know.

"I don't know him," the other guy said.

"How about his barrack number?"

"I have no idea."

Complain to the sarge? Nah, he'd only yell about getting the damn job done. Can I track down that asshole FNG, cold-cock his ass and maybe piss on him for good measure? "Damn it," I said. "We'll need to clean this up."

"It ain't fair," the other guy said. "Why do I need to clean it up?"

I'm not in the mood for whining. "I ain't thrilled about this, either, but the faster we get this done, the quicker we're out of here," I said. *What could I do if he mutinies, too?*

I laid down the mop and broom when I reported the job completed to sarge, but vowed I wouldn't forget that piss-perp. With no idea when, if ever, I'd run across that FNG again, I remained on the lookout. Maybe I'd break his face if I did.

* * *

A sergeant, new to me, selected a handful of FNGs from my barracks, me included. "You, come with me," he said in a matter-of-fact tone.

He walked us to the latrines. "Okay, you cherries, listen up." He gestured with one hand, "You're going to the rear of every latrine and drag the waste receptacle from below the seat opening. Pour kerosene into the barrels and light it."

Fuck.

"You'll need to stir it to get everything to burn," he said. "Add more kerosene if you want."

Oh, what fun. After five months of army training and being flown halfway to nowhere, there I stood, ordered to cook shit.

Shovels, accompanied by several fuel cans and a pile of work gloves, lay on the ground next to the sergeant.

"Any questions?" he asked. "Grab what you need and get to work. I'll check on you in a few minutes."

I laid claim to a pair of gloves.

"Damn, what do they think we are, slaves?" somebody bitched.

I flanked my chosen outhouse, lifted its rear hatch, and dragged out the rust-coated half of a fifty-five-gallon barrel.

God almighty. If the stench of shit wasn't bad enough, the sight of it was worse.

A string of cans, scattered along a line behind the latrines, spewed coal-black soot that only added to the stink.

Somebody gagged.

Upwind, I held my breath, ran up to my can, avoided looking inside while I stirred, then backed off. I thought better about making a run for the tall grass beyond the wire perimeter. Instead, I hovered close by. *Can't accuse me of neglect of duty or attempted desertion.*

Thirty minutes of the smell of burnt shit and fuel made mucking a stable or street-sweeping horse hockey behind a parade in the States seem like coffee with a doughnut.

The sergeant returned and examined the receptacles. "Okay, looks good to me. Put the cans back, leave your equipment here, then you're done."

No fucking gratitude? In the army, it's always do as you're told.

Not able to clean myself fast enough, I showered, gargled, and put on fresh fatigues. Would've flushed my lungs and stomach if I could've.

Unless Charlie attacked, my immediate concern? Get the hell out of Camp Shit-Burn.

* * *

I thought I deserved a rest on my bunk after my sacrifice at the excremental alter, but a voice interrupted that.

"Listen up," somebody demanded.

Everybody's attention refocused on a corporal I'd never seen before.

"Turn in your field jackets," he demanded. "We're collecting them. They're needed and will get redistributed in the field."

Poor slobs in the field must be in a bad way.

A pile of field jackets grew on the floor as FNGs followed the order and surrendered theirs one by one.

* * *

Several hours later, our barrack sergeant checked in. "How are things going?"

"Where are our field jackets going, Sergeant?" one guy asked.

"What do you mean?" Sarge said.

"We turned them in," another FNG responded.

"What?"

"We were told to turn them in for redistribution in the field," someone said.

Our collective heads bobbed.

"Who told you that?" Sarge said.

"We don't know his name," the same FNG replied.

Since my arrival, different corporals and sergeants had appeared, ordered things done, then disappeared. With FNGs all over the place—ants in olive-green fatigues, and me one of them—I couldn't keep track of names, ranks, or faces. Everything and everyone blurred together, replaceable parts in the army machinery.

"That's bullshit," he bellowed. "Don't give your issued gear to anybody."

Hell, how could I know? How many times have I been told to follow orders? My field jacket destined for redistribution ... on the black market, and me, a victim of W. C. Fields's dictum: Never give a sucker an even break. "Asshole lied to us, straight-faced," I grumbled to the guy next to me. "Thieving bastard. I thought we were all on the same side." *What's next, a shiv in the back?* I added, "Watch your back, dude."

Served a 'Nam-style hazing without hand holding, I decided I'd put in my time, navigate the gauntlet, and pray that my ass didn't get blown off before other cherries replaced me at the bottom of the shit-pile. My naïve notions about American purity of purpose and moral superiority—the idealistic beliefs that I'd grown up with and accepted about being American—had been laid bare. Despite everything I'd heard or seen growing up, I'd believed that we were one people, unified, and that we could and would set aside individual differences when in extreme circumstances. But while dismayed, I faced the reality on a deeper emotional level that many of us American soldiers didn't have each other's backs in what I'd thought was our common cause in Vietnam.

Welcome to 'Nam, Dorothy. How the hell did I end up here? I knew exactly—and had no one to blame but myself, though I still raged over being drafted.

HOME, SWEET HOME?

Four days in-country, I'd boarded a military transport in Long Binh headed north. I was somewhat, though not entirely, reassured by my assignment to Two Corps Headquarters. While relieved to escape that in-processing hellhole, Camp Shit-Burn, I regretted I hadn't found that FNG who'd pissed in the corner. Perhaps it was better that I hadn't.

A guy in fatigues with my rank approached me after I stepped off the plane in Nha Trang. "Are you Hogan?"

I determined him a friendly one-man welcoming committee. "Yeah."

"Hi, call me Steve," he said, hand out, with a big smile. Taller than me. Slight southern twang. "We expected you on that plane. I'm here to take you to Headquarters."

"Where're you from, Steve?"

"Mayfield, Missouri. Southeast corner. You?"

"Louisville. Home of bourbon, fast women, and beautiful horses." I hefted my duffle bag containing everything I'd brought, mostly army-issue.

"My kind of town." He grinned.

I followed him to a jeep. "How long have you been in-country?"

"Five months, give or take. I try not to think about that."

Near halfway through his one-year tour. I couldn't imagine myself in the same position. "Haven't started a countdown?"

"No. It'll happen in its own time."

"I can't believe my assignment here," I said. "I'd feared spending a year at a battalion firebase outpost. I expect Corps Headquarters means high-ranking officers, a euphemism for safe."

"Yeah, a good assignment. We'll stop off at 55th Military Intelligence Detachment Headquarters. Once you're signed in, we'll head to our office at Corps Headquarters. Stick with me; I'll show you the ropes."

Steve slid into a comfortable groove in my mind, an unused big-brother niche—an equal I could look to for support, who wouldn't bullshit me or take advantage.

I kept an interested eye on our surroundings, including the blond-colored beach on our right, hard to miss, beyond the single row of palms that lined that side of the two-lane street. *But ... aren't we easy targets in an open jeep?*

* * *

"Hogan reporting," I told the clerk at Detachment Headquarters, a small one-story house shaded by palm trees with an otherwise unobstructed view of the beach.

"Ah, you're here," he said.

Did I have a choice?

Within a few minutes, the clerk had completed some paperwork. "Sign here and you're done. Report to your Corps Headquarters office."

* * *

Steve turned our jeep left out of our unit's compound and a fruity smell confronted me, pungent and sweet, something I couldn't place—something not familiar in Kentucky. *Rotting bananas or mangoes?*

"Hey, you ever go to that beach, Steve?"

"Yeah, head out there all the time for a little Frisbee and football." He slowed the jeep for another left turn. "You interested?"

"Yeah," I said, but then caught myself. "Is it safe?"

"Usually."

What the hell does that mean?

Guard towers stood at each corner of a ten-foot chain-link fence, lined along the top with concertina wire, barbwire on steroids, a.k.a. razor wire. One good look at it made me cringe.

Steve guided the jeep past the guard at the gate. "This is it, Two Corps Headquarters. You'll like it here."

"I sure the fuck hope so."

"We call this 'the Compound' and that," Steve pointed to the imposing pale-yellow building to our left, "'is the French Hotel.'"

I spotted another chain-link fence, straight ahead about eighty yards, and a street beyond. Then, I inventoried the compound. Various buildings created a central open area, which was covered with gravel and otherwise occupied by several large, leafy trees. "How big is this postage stamp, anyway?"

"About ten acres, surrounded by city neighborhoods. Everything's provided here at Headquarters: barracks, doctor and dental offices, a mess hall, an Enlisted Men's Club, even an outdoor movie theater." Steve grinned. "Well, everything except women." He parked the jeep near an A-frame sheet-metal-roofed barrack with wooden slats and screens along its sides, and about sixty feet from the Headquarters building. "Here we are ... home, sweet home. Grab your bag."

The barrack's spring-hinged screen door, flung open by Steve, slammed shut behind us, *Clack!*

The space inside, from the bare concrete floor to the roof, as well as the gray-painted wood slats that covered the outside halfway up, suited a hot, humid climate, different from any barrack I'd seen at Fort Knox, Fort Holabird, or Camp Shit-Burn. A row of bunks lined each side, about twenty in all, creating a wide central aisle down the middle. Fans and lights hung from beams across the open ceiling, everything turned off. I noticed another screen door at the other end.

"No crowding. Plenty of room to move in a hurry," I said.

I followed Steve's hand signal, then spied the unoccupied bunk near the entrance. "Try that bunk and store your things in an empty locker there," he said.

A bank of enameled-gray lockers stood several feet away.

"Okay. No Basic and AIT upper-bunk nose-bleeders." I chuckled. My duffle bag dropped on the empty bunk, I spotted an open door on one of the nearest lockers and pointed. "I'll take that one."

"Everybody here belongs to our unit and works around Headquarters Compound. Some work in the vans parked here. They compile weekly and monthly summary reports that go to MACV in Saigon."

"Military Assistance Command, Vietnam?" I asked to make sure I understood.

"Yeah. Other guys study aerial photos. I think several guys intercept radio transmissions here, too."

The exposed rafters overhead created open space. Steve's words echoed between the corrugated sheet metal roof and smooth, unpainted concrete floor, which created a sense of emptiness for me. "Take a few minutes to get settled in before we go up to the office." He waved one hand. "No rush."

"Okay, Steve. This beats the hell out of a dirt hole covered with sandbags." *I might be able to spend time writing to Pam, or relaxing and getting to know these guys, rather than spending time dodging sniper fire and mortar rounds.* But I felt resolved to do anything to get me through the coming year. *Just leave 'Nam alive.*

* * *

Two weeks before the end of AIT in Baltimore, during a jaunt to Washington, DC, I'd met Pam at the Crazy Horse Saloon. I had been desperate for a connection with a woman and luckily the nightclub hadn't carded me. No clue why, but I certainly hadn't argued that point with them.

Pam's rounded cheeks and shoulder-length brunette ponytail attracted me, like a bee to a blossom. She was on a girls' night out, and I was likely friendlier than others, so she responded in kind, which was a welcome encouragement. She invited me to sit with them after we'd danced.

Willing to climb into her panties at closing time, but lacking the skills of subtlety, and without the courage to be blunt, I asked for her phone number, and she gave it to me.

We talked on the phone once or twice, but, typical in the story of my life, I graduated AIT with orders for 'Nam before I reached second base with her.

Pam lived six hundred miles from Louisville and I'd dismissed the possibility of a visit with her during my leave, though fantasized about sex with her every day. Writing her from 'Nam might keep us connected.

* * *

My territory marked with a few items of gear on the bunk, I placed my khakis, two additional sets of fatigues, an extra pair of boots, and a folded duffle bag into the empty locker.

Steve lay stretched out on the bunk across the aisle, face up and eyes closed, head cradled in clasped hands.

Bphbphpbh!

The loud, steady noise nearby riveted my attention. *A lawn mower? Surely, not. Not on gravel, anyway.*

39

A white mist billowed in through the screen as the noise moved by and brought the smell of oil and an acrid taste, unnatural, man-made.

"Blah. What the hell?"

Steve stirred. "A little bug spray."

"War on bugs," I mumbled. My new locker secured with a personal padlock, I said in a raised voice, "Ready to go."

As we crossed the gravel toward the Headquarters building, I watched the small truck, driven by a frail-looking Vietnamese male, some thirty yards distance, as it moved away from us. The pith helmet he wore swayed from side to side, along with his head, as the vehicle bounced over uneven gravel. The noisy machine rested on the truck bed and spewed a thick blue-white cloud. The smoke, blown out the back faster than the vehicle moved forward, suggested an inefficient rocket motor.

* * *

Our footsteps on the beige linoleum floor and up the wide stairwell to the second floor echoed inside the Hotel. Hard not to take note of the colonial architecture. The high ceilings, wide corridors, large windows, and walls painted pale yellow created a bright and airy space, unlike any military headquarters I'd ever seen.

At the top of the stairs, Steve pointed straight ahead. "There's the general's office."

General?

Steve turned left and continued down the hallway, me alongside.

"I've never been near a general, except Eisenhower lying in state at the Capitol," I said. "Afterward I saluted a motorcade in procession along Pennsylvania Avenue toward the White House. Stood at attention on the sidewalk and saluted Nixon near the head of the column, as his limo passed. Saw him through the window, but he didn't even glance my way. It took forever for the rest of the parade to pass. For the first several cars my buddy and I saluted each car, but I said to him, 'What are we doing? Hold your salute until the end.'"

"Any of them return your salutes?"

"Hell, no. I doubt any of those bigwigs even noticed us."

The "French Hotel" in the Two Corps Headquarters compound, as seen from the front entrance gate. (I worked in the upper floor office located above the sign, LIGHTS ON, and with windows partially obscured by a palm frond. As well, I billeted within the compound during the first portion of my 'Nam tour.)

LIFE COMPOUNDED

"Meet Rudy," John said. "You're his replacement. He'll show you your job." With that, John had completed my introduction and tour of the room.

When Steve and I had entered the office, John, an E-6, had taken over my orientation. Aside from his rank, I'd determined John a lifer by the wrinkles on his face and faded army tattoo on one forearm. Not hard to tell he'd seen things. Friendly enough, though. He introduced me to Lieutenant Raines, the man-in-charge of our office, who rose to welcome me with a handshake at his desk. Raines, mid-twenties, a few years older than me, didn't come across as a tight-ass.

"How short are you, Rudy?" I asked, curious how many days before he left 'Nam.

Stockier, a few inches shorter than me, a broad smile crossed his olive-tanned face. "Going back to 'the World' in ten."

"The World" ... a utopia of home and country I'd constructed in my mind, the one place deserving the classification of civilization, the place where I hung my hopes and dreams. Seemed every GI did the same.

"Where exactly?"

"Miami. Land of oranges, Cuba Libres, and bikinis, and I plan to get me some, first thing back."

"You lucky dog."

Without the ocean breezes through open windows and the overhead ceiling fans that crept in slow circles, the moist and heavy air in the office would've congealed into concrete and entombed us within our perspiration. Six analysts positioned on stools in two rows at long tables faced the aisle down the middle of the room. Each had a metal file cabinet positioned within easy reach. The high ceiling countered the sense of the cramped floor area, but tight spaces presented no problem for me; I'd crawled in and out of caves in rural Kentucky during my late-teen years.

Rudy pointed to one of the large tables. "You'll work here." He pulled up another stool and motioned, "Have a seat," then picked up several papers. "If you review your incoming reports every day, you'll make your job easier." He turned and pointed to a large topographic map on the wall behind us. "Up to date as of yesterday."

"Marking up a topo with a grease pencil seemed fun in AIT … not so much now," I said.

"No, but your work supports the Two Corp Officers in planning B-52 Arc-Light bombings, artillery strikes, and infantry search-and-destroy missions."

Unable to see our adversary on the map, much less make eye contact with them, I said, "Charlie's out there, somewhere, moving around in the thousands, beyond the Compound, beyond the city limits of Nha Trang and he wants us out of 'Nam, dead or alive." (We'd shortened the name Viet Cong to VC, from the US Army's phonetic term Victor Charlie, but usually referred to them as Charlie.)

"You're preaching to the choir," Rudy replied.

"I imagine we're on a VC or NVA intelligence analyst's overlay hidden in the Central Highlands jungle somewhere." We referred to North Vietnamese Army regulars as NVA.

"More likely Hanoi." Rudy gave me a head bob. "Follow me. I'll introduce you to Major Gaston. You'll work with him."

Oh, God, mid-level in the officer food chain. "Major?" I hadn't been around majors before. I'd been around lieutenants frequently, captains occasionally, but never majors. *Now, I'm gonna be working for one, face to face?*

"He's not bad. You won't see him every day. He'll inform you when he wants your assistance. You might even get to travel with him. The officers' responsibilities are divided like ours. Each one oversees several provinces within Two Corps. We handle the secretarial part of the intel effort. They report to and advise the Corps CO."

I'm just a glorified gofer.

Six individual desks scattered around a large room demonstrated once again that rank held privileges.

My brief introduction to Gaston went okay, but I didn't relax until Rudy and I left the officers' work area. The major, older and more formal than Raines, had been abrupt and no-nonsense. I concluded he was someone I'd best be careful around.

Despite my qualms about the major, "Well, Rudy, I'll take this any day over a grunt's situation in the boonies," I said.

* * *

Second day in the Compound, cooked chow in my gut and a shower to wash away the day's sweat, I wanted the lay of the land.

"How long have you been here?" I asked one of my new barrack mates while I pulled on a set of civvies.

"On my second tour. I extended one year," he said. Thick, dark-framed glasses accentuated his red-haired crew cut.

"Why another tour, man? Got a death wish?"

"An extra year here and I'll get discharged when I return to 'the World.'"

"Nice to avoid Stateside duty, but another year here? How's it been?"

"Plum. Felt a little shaky during Tet, though."

"The Tet Offensive? Really?" TV images of frantic GIs fighting off Charlie's attacks from eighteen months earlier flashed in my mind, vivid as yesterday's news. "I saw the coverage on TV. Looked like all hell broke loose. Charlie hadn't gained control of much for more than a few days, but won himself a psychological victory."

"Overrated," he said. "We could hear heavy fighting. Were told it was on the north side of Nha Trang across the river around the big Buddha statue."

"Across the river?"

"Yeah, a couple of miles away."

Better there than right outside the Compound fence. "Did anything happen here? At Headquarters, I mean." *VC in the surrounding neighborhood with my serial number on a bullet?* I wanted some idea of my odds of survival as I walked across the graveled compound to and from work, or headed for a shower or a shit.

"One of the compounds nearby took small-arms fire. I heard it from here."

"Oh? Anybody hit? I mean, Americans?"

"No. None of our guys. They weren't overrun and got reinforcements quickly. The firefight ended within a couple of hours."

Clack! Our barrack screen door signaled someone's approach.

Steve stopped, slightly out of breath. "Hey, guys, let's go get a drink."

"Where you been?" I asked.

"Babysitter duty for 'the old man.'"

I knew Steve referred to the general.

My new mate took a breath. "I got other stuff to do."

I figured our conversation had concluded. "I'm in, Steve. Give me a sec," I said and finished tying my shoelaces.

Ahead of me, Steve swung the screen door open.

"How's it look?" I asked. "A cluster of officers anywhere? I detest saluting them. Got no choice … that's what burns my buns."

"I don't mind." Steve glanced at me and grinned. "Makes them a juicier target than me."

"Damn good point, fella."

As we crossed the Compound, halfway to the Enlisted Men's Club, I spotted several figures. "Are those officers? We're on a collision course."

"Hard to tell. Probably not. The officers scurry around during daylight and get scarce at night. I figure officers and cockroaches balance each other out in the universe."

"False alarm," I said as we passed several enlisted guys.

The noise from inside the club grew louder as we approached and when we opened the door, a shock wave of "Proud Mary" blasted us head-on.

The band's amplified noise all but obliterated the young singer's voice, her English words in an accent not quite Vietnamese.

Steve and I claimed opposite chairs at a small, empty table and I noticed the absence of other females in the room.

My eardrums ached. I looked at Steve and raised my voice. "Jeez, this band sounds like cats in heat."

I watched Steve's lips. "Yeah, but what to do?" He tapped his watch with a finger. "It's getting a little late to go into town. Too much rush to get back before curfew."

"You mean we can go into town?"

"Yeah, but we need to return by ten."

"I'm sure she's doing the best she can," I said, referring to the singer, my justification for a continued presence in the club and reconciliation to spending a lot of evenings in that joint. I gave her another once-over. Her shoulder-length, straight dark hair swayed as she moved. Not knockout gorgeous, but she had the right equipment and was worth a gawk. I'd have been happy to escort her to a darkened, quiet place for some personal groping.

Steve shrugged and raised his eyebrows. His lips moved again and I strained to hear what I guessed was his closest approximation of a Yiddish accent. "And she's getting paid for it."

When the song ended and I could hear normal shouting again. "I think the 'Proud Mary' sprang a leak and sank."

"I've heard worse," Steve quipped.

"Beats hanging around my bunk, I guess. At least I can get drunk, stagger the few yards to bed, and fantasize screwing her or my girlfriend, Pam."

"Better than having a sharp stick poked in your eye," Steve said.

No escape from reminders of home, everything I saw—compared and found lacking—summed up 'Nam.

"Vodka and orange," I told the male waiter.

When the guy served my drink, I paid in MPCs and waved my remaining bills at Steve. "Monopoly money. Doesn't feel right." Not allowed to use greenbacks in-country, I'd surrendered mine as ordered during 'Nam in-processing and received an equivalent handful of "Military Payment Certificates" in exchange.

"I can't get no … satisfaction … ," the singer belted out.

"Me, neither," I mouthed back at her.

"Funny money," Steve yelled. "I'll take it if you don't want it." He chuckled.

"That's all right, I'll figure out how to get rid of it." I downed my heavy-sweet neon-orange mix. Not orange juice as I'd expected.

When my second plastic cup of elixir arrived, I yelled to Steve, "Medicinal purposes." Then I forced down another nauseating swallow, an essential substance to loosen the vise-like grip my surroundings had on my mind. A constant awareness that wherever I went or whatever I did, an attack could occur—who knew what, when, how—while homesickness, the emotional equivalent of gravity, threatened to grind me into the dirt.

48

I'd told myself umpteen times not to order another glass of syrup. Hadn't worked. I wondered if I'd slipped into Dad's shoes, his drinking not a pretty picture as I'd grown up.

* * *

I had laid on the booze with Alex, Wade, and Jellybean during AIT.

Alex's openness caught my attention on my first day there, even before he approached me with two other guys and introduced himself. I'd watched him talking and joking, and envied him for that.

"Hi, I'm Alex, from El Paso. Tex-Mex," he'd said. White teeth against his tanned face highlighted a broad smile.

"I noticed you earlier, Alex," I said.

He glanced to his right. "This is Wade, a New Mexico farm boy." Glanced to his left. "This is Jeff. Oklahoma. I call him Jellybean."

I sized them up as we shook hands. Alex was social, confident, a natural leader. Wade, darker-skinned, appeared to be a reserved follower. Mixed heritage? I didn't ask. That didn't matter to me, anyway. Jellybean, a pale, white, crew-cut redhead on the timid side, could sunburn in a heartbeat. He was easygoing, with the air of an eager puppy. I could relate to Jellybean as if we were twins.

Alex continued, "I met these jokers in Basic at Fort Bliss, an infernal oven, dry and dusty country, swarming with cowpoke-rednecks." He chuckled and glanced at them. "Present company excluded."

"Any of you guys have a car here?" I said. *If just one of us had a car, we could roam when "off duty."*

"Didn't get the chance to bring mine," Alex answered.

"No," said Wade.

Jellybean shook his head.

"Damn, me neither," I said. *It's Verlon's now, anyway.*

When Friday's classes ended, Alex approached me. "Want to join Wade, Jellybean, and me for a drink, tonight?"

Without a sister and with only brief visits with cousins, I'd grown up with few chances to interact with girls, other than in school. As a result, I viewed girls with awe and curiosity, and damn near considered them a different species. I'd hoped during adolescence that a girl would over-power my shyness and force herself upon me, so that sex would play a direct, personal role in my life. But no! I'd plodded a tortured solitary path that had consumed me for seven years. Comfortable around booze, however, I jumped in with both feet. "Sure."

"Well then, let's buy a bottle of something." Alex looked at me. "What's your poison? We drank sloe gin at Bliss."

Wade spoke up. "Tequila's good."

"I can't stand hard stuff," I said. "I've gotten sicker than a dog on whiskey and gin more than once."

"Sloe gin then?" Alex asked me. "Okay with you, Jellybean?"

Jellybean nodded.

"I'll give it a whirl," I said.

* * *

We had roosted on a darkened hill on base, away from the direct glare of a streetlight, a replay of similar scenes from my teenage years.

After a good part of the bottle was consumed, unabashed, Alex asked me, "You a virgin?"

That caught me off guard. *No need to hide anything from these guys.* I'd long ago adjusted to my nakedness in front of other guys in open showers from junior high onward. "Yeah, ain't got none, yet."

"Well, join the crowd. I ain't either," he said.

My admission didn't ease my horniness, but at least in their presence, I wasn't a one-off mutant. "Can't talk to women very well," I said. "Never figured out how to do that."

"Can't do with them, can't do without them," Wade said.

Ready to burst at the thought of a young, soft, female body against mine, I looked at our communal font of liquid anesthesia. "Pass that over to me." The smooth, sweet swallow warmed me on the way down, without the shudder and caustic burn of whiskey or gin.

"I'll take another hit," Alex said. He took a swig, then passed the bottle along, "Here, Jellybean."

Quiet, Jellybean looked embarrassed.

"Spill it, Jellybean," I said. "Don't lie. You a virgin?"

He nodded.

After that, we'd spent most weekend nights passing bottles of sloe gin, a poor substitute for the closeness of a woman, and I failed to dilute my male hormones, horny and obsessed as ever.

* * *

Now, as the band took a break, I noticed my ears rang.

Steve's lips moved. I heard his faint words, "I need to take a leak. Back in a shake."

Alone at the table, both hands around my milky-white plastic glass of vodka and syrupy orange soda, I thought about the time Mom insisted I roust Dad from a bar. I recalled being about thirteen at the time.

"Do I have to?" I'd asked her.

"I won't go into a beer joint," Mom had responded. "You go."

When I'd entered, Dad sat on a bar stool talking to a woman next to him, and both were faced away from the door. I walked up, stood at his other side, shoulder height, and blurted, "Mom wants you to come home now."

I'd studied Dad's expression for clues, had caught him by surprise, feared he'd backhand me ... considered myself lucky when he didn't.

My recollection interrupted, I looked up to see Steve returning to his seat.

"That's better," Steve said. "You know most GIs in 'Nam would envy our situation here at Corps Headquarters."

"Yeah, from the bigger picture, my enlistment to become an Intel Analyst three days after my conscription appears a good choice. But hell, can't I hope for anything better? Can't I entertain an escape from this shit-pile?" *Me, a cork on an angry ocean of churning waves and howling winds.*

"A little tail might fix that." Steve flashed a mischievous grin.

BURN, BABY, BURN

"I've finished updating the duty roster," John told me. "Your turn to burn the classified trash." He tapped one finger on the clipboard he held, then pointed to a hook on the wall. "I post the roster there, next to the burn-cage key."

I spotted said key, dangling by a string from a fist-sized piece of wood.

"Steve, show Connard the drill," John said.

My third day in the office and already assigned to a work detail.

Steve jumped from his stool. "Sure thing." He snatched the wood from the hook and the key danced on the end of the string as Steve crossed the floor.

Before I laid down the report I held, Steve stood in front of me, cocked his head toward the door, then said, "Come on, bud. Let's go burn something." He winked and flashed his familiar grin.

I hefted our large dingy-white cloth bag about the size of a duffle and full to the brim, slung it over my shoulder, and followed. I didn't mind going with him. Steve was always up for a bit of fun from what I'd gathered, and I felt more at ease around him than anyone else there. And anyway, we wouldn't be under the watchful eye of higher-ups.

"What's in here anyway?" I asked as we headed down the hallway.

"Unwanted CONFIDENTIAL trash," Steve said. "Though now and then a few of my papers marked SECRET have crawled in." He grinned. "Oops."

We exited the Hotel through the back entrance, the crunch of gravel replacing echoes of hard-sole boots within the building.

"Where're we headed, Steve?"

"The burn enclosure's over there, past our hooch." He pointed in the direction of our enlisted-man's latrine.

* * *

When Steve and I rounded the corner between our barrack and latrine entrance, five older Vietnamese men, each wearing a badge—workers, who I took to be grounds keepers—squatted against the back wall. Their loose-fitting clothing and wrinkled faces suggested they shrank with each breath. A strong smell of vinegar and steamed vegetables, mixed with a tinge of rotted fish, and the small empty metal containers with chopsticks next to them, suggested a lunch break. One guy spat dark juice on the ground.

A few steps on, I asked Steve, "Did you see that? What did he spit?"

"Betel nut juice. They don't swallow the stuff. Their version of chewing tobacco, betel nut gives them a buzz and prevents tooth decay. Turns their chompers black, though. Imagine … they consider black teeth a look of beauty."

"In Kentucky, we always considered darkened teeth a sign of impoverished neglect."

Steve stopped and, preparing to open a padlock, said, "We've arrived."

Exiled to the back corner of the Compound. Up against the perimeter chain-link fence. Out of sight … and out of the minds of everyone else at Headquarters.

A second chain-link fence enclosed a square concrete pad about twelve feet on the side, covered by a metal roof that came to a point in the center.

These fences won't stop shit.

Steve turned the key in the padlock on the secured gate. *Click!* "Always make sure to lock the gate when you leave."

"Understood."

Those fences wouldn't stop bullets from an AK-47—Charlie's favorite weapon—nor grenade fragments. They'd keep out a rabid dog, but wouldn't stop a spray of cuss words or a dirty look from an angry local.

I had learned while growing up that shit happened, sometimes bad shit. Mom, Verlon, and I couldn't predict when Dad would come home late on Fridays after work, how drunk he'd be, or how wild and violent he'd get. And I had no reason to believe Charlie would be any more predictable.

I recalled John showing me an M-1 carbine soon after my arrival and saying, "We keep this in the office and use it without need to draw a weapon from the arms locker. Avoids paperwork."

"Got it, Sarge," I'd said. Getting a weapon out of the arms locker, as far as I imagined, would've required a figurative check of my rectum, answering a barrage of questions, and my signature in triplicate. Maybe, the guy in charge would've ridiculed me for wanting a weapon inside the Compound, if for no other reason than because my request caused him paperwork.

"Hey, Steve, why didn't we bring the M-1 rifle from the office?"

"No need," Steve said as he opened the enclosure gate and entered, "This place has never been on Charlie's dance card, bro. Probably, anyway. Besides, a carbine wouldn't do you much good. You do understand that the small ammo clips for our M-1 carbine limit its ability to compete with an AK on automatic? The one who throws the most lead the fastest in a firefight gains the advantage."

I followed him into the enclosure. *Equivalent to defending myself with paper wads?*

"Okay, let's get this bonfire going," Steve said. "Dump the bag and give it a light."

I emptied the bag's contents of unwanted intel papers onto a pile of ash mixed with small amounts of charred paper in the middle of the floor. Disturbed, fine particles filled the air. *Ptui!* I tried not to inhale, and forced enough air out of my lungs to say, "I don't have a match."

Steve pulled a Bic from a pocket. "Use this."

I touched a corner of yellow paper poking from the middle of the pile. A tiny flame spread, more smoke than fire.

"It'll burn faster if you move it around." Steve reached for a rake leaning against the fence, then offered it to me.

Aw, damn, not going to help? "How long does it take?"

"Give or take, thirty minutes."

With a firm grip, I accepted the implement. "Anything to get this done quicker. This mound of flat papers will likely smolder, go out, and lie there till snakes grow legs, without some encouragement. The pile would burn faster if we doused the fucker with diesel."

Steve didn't budge, hummed a few notes of what I recognized as "Light My Fire" before he stopped. "Oh, you mean, a righteous fire?" he said. "No, I don't know where we'd get the juice. Besides, I suspect the officers are scared shit-less we'd burn down the Compound."

I pictured myself engulfed in flames, recalled the Buddhist monk I'd seen on TV before I knew I'd end up in 'Nam. The guy sat down in a busy street intersection, had another monk douse him and light a match. Poof! He hadn't flinched. What had it taken for him to do that?

Smoke drifted into my eyes. The first whiff reminded me of the smell of rags my grandparents burned to ward off mosquitoes, but that was incense compared with the stench of burning shit. *Cough!* I squinted, waved my free hand, jockeyed a few steps to get fresh air, and inhaled a quick breath.

Little chance of suffocation. The smoke had ample opportunity to escape through the fence and the vent in the roof, but no, rather than go the hell away, it lingered inside the enclosure.

"The most important thing is to burn all the paper," Steve said. With his arms folded across his chest and one leg across the other, he leaned against the fence.

"Yeah, you never know" I stabbed at the pile "who might want to rummage through our burned trash for some exciting reading."

"Speaking of which, I've got a prime collection of girlie mags you can borrow, whenever. I'd trust you not to paste any of the pages together."

Loan me his nudie mags? A real friend. "Well, Steve, I may take you up on that at some point," I said, and filed his offer away.

He glanced at a push broom propped against the fence. "When you're done burning, sweep the ashes into a pile in the middle." He looked on in silence for a few moments as I repositioned the papers, then stirred from his restful position. "Well, appears you've got this weenie roast under control. I'll leave you the key."

"Got somewhere more important to be?" I dared not say that I wanted him to stick around to keep me company, watch my back, and bullshit with me. Didn't want him to think me a wuss.

"Catch up on my beauty sleep." He grinned. "John won't expect either of us back for a while. Take your time."

"Yeah, sure," I said. *Easy for you to say, about to enjoy private time with the latest Playboy centerfold. Me? Rake in hand, and only separated from the street by smoke and wire, maybe I could counterattack Charlie with my gardening implement.*

"See you later," he said.

The key stuffed into my front pocket, I watched Steve disappear from view, whistling "Light My Fire" as he went. I noticed the workers had cleared out, too. I took a long look at the houses up and down the dusty, potholed street across from my position. Heard no one, saw no one.

Focusing again on my exhibition fire dance, I made sure to face the street or, at least, keep it in my peripheral vision. How many guys had died in 'Nam while gassing a jeep, shining their boots, or wiping their asses? One shot from a passing motorbike, that's all it would take. Me, trapped inside a fenced enclosure and shot execution-style … there one minute and gone the next. My chest tightened. *Dying from a bullet isn't good, no matter the circumstances, because dead is dead.*

I recalled what had happened to Aunt Betty and Uncle Tunney. Uncle Tunney had taken a gun to Aunt Betty, then to himself. From Mom's reaction, that had been the worst day of her life. And, from what I saw, my grandparents as well. Everybody on Mom's side of my family was stunned. Worst day of my life, too, until I'd been dragged into the army.

At twelve years old, I couldn't figure out what to make of Uncle Tunney's actions. He'd always been kind and generous around me. I knew he'd worked as an ambulance driver for a while and heard him talk about that. I wondered how that had affected him. I now think Uncle Tunney had an accumulation of trauma from witnessing personal injury and death when tending to others on the job and, coupled with his marital separation, lacked a healthy outlet to deal with all that.

When Uncle Tunney and Aunt Betty died, I'd stayed quiet. Hadn't cried. Wanted to keep my shame secret. Hadn't wanted my friends to find out, either. What would they think of my family? What would they think of me?

I raked, watched the fire … smelled the burnt-paper smoke. *What had happened to Uncle Tunney for him to have done that?* I still hadn't arrived at a satisfactory answer.

I poked at the pile. "Come on, burn, damn you."

Unburned scraps hid within the charred remains. I surmised not everyone held a high degree of enthusiasm for completing their burn duty.

A motorbike revved in the distance.

I spread the pile, mixed charred and smoldering papers with fresh ones, reshuffling everything. Careful to maintain my view of the street, I backed off, unable to avoid the lazy smoke for more than a few seconds.

The motorbike engine and successive gear shifts grew louder.

What could I do if things went south? No cover for twenty feet, I'd first need to escape the burn cage.

The cycle close by, I faced the street, rake at the ready.

A guy, mid-twenties maybe, bobbed up and down as he rode into and out of potholes that peppered the street. He sported a bright-colored plaid short-sleeve shirt—a pattern you'd never catch me wearing—and faded blue jeans. His forward concentration suggested he wasn't Charlie, instead a working stiff on a lunch break or errand. But Charlie wore whatever he wanted and I wouldn't know the difference. Restaurant cook by day, mortar squad leader by night.

Assured he hadn't stopped nearby, I turned my attention back to my fire.

"Hurry up, burn, damn it." Would a Vietnamese smoke spirit … or burn god … hear my plea and take pity? I raked and watched. Nothing changed, as far as I could tell. The paper resisted my efforts despite me.

Slow progress, I left nothing behind to read.

The flame out, I swept the smoldering remains of ash and embers into a neat little mound in the center of the floor. I paused with a deep breath, as if in meditation, and studied the street. Knew subsequent fires would turn that ash to gas, and all the gas would drift away, like parts of my past, things I'd never do again, people I'd never see again.

Gate locked, I got the hell out of there before Charlie appeared with a gun, and on my way back to the office I noticed I reeked of smoke. With a glance at my watch, I calculated my burn job had taken forty-five minutes. *Well, at least it isn't as bad as burning shit.*

LIFE'S A BEACH

A couple of days later, released from the office at five, I headed out the rear exit of the Hotel to catch a breeze.

Bphbphpbh!

It was impossible to miss the sound of that same little, wrinkled Vietnamese driver, equipped with pith helmet, who focused dead ahead and didn't flinch, trailed by a thick white cloud.

On a collision course, I paused. "Come on, hurry up, I don't have all day." I knew the old man couldn't hear me as his machine drowned out my voice.

Engulfed in the muggy, thick air, and on the verge of melting, I felt the sweat, hidden under my fatigues, roll down my arms, chest, and legs. Gravel underfoot crunched as I shifted my weight and waited for the vehicle to pass.

"Finally," I complained and lunged into the smoke bank toward my barrack.

Small droplets, cool and oily, collected on my bare skin. Within several steps my diaphragm verged on a spasm and with a mind of its own, I sucked in a lungful of the cloud.

Cough! Hack, hack! I waved my arms, like that would help, and hurried forward through the vapor. *This shit could kill me.*

I lay on my bunk to clear my head. *Hack!*

Steve rushed in, straight for his bunk, fatigue blouse unbuttoned. "Hey, bud, let's hit the beach and throw some football."

The beach, outside our guarded sanctuary, could be a dangerous place. Although risking it seemed better than inhaling toxic fumes or enduring stark-raving-fucking boredom.

"Dad drove my family a thou—" *Cough!*, "a thousand miles to a beach in Florida for a week's vacation once." *Cough!* "You say you've gone out there before, Steve?"

"Yeah, all the time. Come on, let's go."

"Give me a minute." I foraged through my locker until I found my swim trunks, which I'd buried under my dirty laundry.

I noticed Steve's ID badge clipped to his trunks. "Need my badge?"

"Don't leave home without it."

I gave the gate guard a nod. He nodded back, but otherwise appeared indifferent as we sashayed through the gate on our way to what I hoped would be beach heaven, a couple of stone-throws away, each with a towel and ID, clad in trunks and flip-flops, prepared to soak up some sun. I glanced at Steve. "Well, that was easy."

"Yeah, you can come and go as you please. I leave the Compound most every day."

"Easy enough to go AWOL. But though the army's a threat to my sanity, Charlie's a threat to my life, and my mama didn't raise any fools." I picked up my pace. "Damn, this asphalt's hot." Walking under the July sun in the late afternoon felt like a trip through a steam bath. I'd have sworn I saw water vapor rise in the air. Once in the sand on the other side of the road, I continued, "It won't be hard to avoid the trash strewn about, but what about hidden pull tabs and broken glass?"

"You gets what you pays for," Steve replied. "Wear your foot-treads across the loose stuff near the road. No problem on the wet-pack by the water."

After a forty-yard stretch through wavy, loose blond-brown sand, though still within yelling distance of the guard gate, Steve spread out his multicolored beach towel. "Here's good."

We spread ourselves with sunscreen lotion to prevent sunburn, though we didn't want to be four-limbed marshmallows. Puffs of cloud hung motionless in the sky like pictures on walls. My feet had wanted a breather all day and made love to the warm sand. The rhythm of the breaking waves and the rumble of small pebbles herded by advancing and retreating water drowned out the faded noises of light traffic along the street. The few people scattered along the length of the gentle-sloping beach appeared absorbed in their activities and were uninterested in us.

My senses encouraged me to relax and enjoy ... the warm sand, the smell of salty air, and the anticipated chill of cool water to come. I scanned the ocean horizon where the blue sky should meet blue water. Instead, a milky haze blended into a dingy hue where the farthest boats searched for a day's fish catch or maybe they were running guns or ferrying Charlie. I felt thankful I wouldn't need to board them to determine their purpose. I felt thankful I didn't need to hump a heavy pack on patrols through a jungle full of mosquitoes, venomous snakes, and leeches, nor eat cold C-rations for dinner.

But Charlie could wait on the beach, disguised, for a GI sap to present him with a perfect target. Steve and I hadn't been guaranteed safety. We could catch a sniper bullet in the back from a passing vehicle or one of the numerous rooftops, or encounter a grenade tossed from under loose-fitting clothing.

I looked south at rocky cliffs about two miles distant. "What's down that way, Steve?"

"Cam Ranh Bay, about twenty-five miles straight shot down the coast."

I looked north. "How about that way?"

"The Cai River crosses the beach about a mile up." Steve pointed. "Keep going past those cliffs there, North Vietnam."

North Vietnam? "How far?"

"I'd say four hundred miles."

Pam lived farther away from Louisville than that! "How safe are we here at Corps Headquarters?"

"Safer than screwing a leprous gorilla with a condom," Steve replied.

"Well, don't sugarcoat it, dude." I knew Steve didn't have that answer, couldn't reassure me of anything any more than I could reassure Mom. With a suggested wave of the football, I said, "Steve, go out for a pass."

Steve returned the favor, then pointed, "Throw it to me before I hit the water."

Meh. My effort wasn't a tight spiral.

Steve stretched out, secured a grip on the ball, then collided with a three-foot breaker. Sea foam churned, water ran inland up the gently sloped beach, and the wave's fury played out. Steve staggered to his feet, wiping his face with one hand while clutching the ball with the other.

"Good catch," I said. "Hit me."

The agitated mix of churning seawater with its bubbles and sand tumbled me and forced my face against the bottom. Eyelids squeezed tight, I clutched the ball. *One second, two seconds, three ... I'll drown if I don't get to my feet.*

I fought to stand, then sputtered and gulped air as I staggered a few steps from the water's edge. "I need a sec," I yelled. Shook my head to clear my ears of sand. Wiped water away from around my burning eyes. My nose and throat stung and a wave of nausea threatened a public barf-fest.

"Okay, coffee break's over, throw me another one," Steve yelled.

I reveled in my receiving abilities against the washing machine of seawater, reminded of my dreams of football in junior and high school training programs.

Never invited to try out, I'd approached my high school football coach about playing on our varsity team before the beginning of my senior year.

He'd dismissed me with the quip, "Not unless you can run forty yards in four-and-a-half flat in full gear."

No way I could've done that in four-and-a-half seconds.

A second cousin, on the team and next to me, had jumped in, "But Coach, he's good."

That didn't change Coach's mind. He didn't bother to ask questions to determine my skills or suggest I suit up and show him what I could do on the receiving end of a football. Didn't care.

That had crushed my high school football dreams, though they'd limped on in fantasy.

Steve started toward his blanket. "I'm tired. Let's quit."

"One more time," I said.

Steve heaved the ball.

With a quick sprint to one side and a reach over my shoulder, I made the connection. Loose sand pressed between my toes, shifted under my feet and I stumbled face-first. After I picked myself up, I looked at Steve and said, "The touchdown stands and the fans are going wild."

"Yeah. Hogan laid himself out and paid for it with a hard hit," Steve responded.

"Made for a great comeback finish, though." I brushed off and collected my things.

Steve smiled. "Looking forward to seeing more great plays by that promising young receiver."

We fought our way across the loose sand between us and the road, while a conical straw hat bobbed on a mission to intercept us. Two baskets, suspended and balanced on a long pole, bounced in rhythm to quick, labored steps.

"What's that wiry woman up to?" I asked Steve.

She pulled up in our path, rested her baskets on the sand, and made eye contact with me. "You buy?"

I waved her off. "No, not today."

She flashed a frown.

"Hey, I want to show you something," Steve told me. He looked at her and pointed to a wicker basket.

A lifted lid released wisps of water vapor from the basket and revealed a clutch of eggs.

Steve nodded to her and indicated with a pointed finger, "That one."

Purchase in hand, Steve stopped at the road's edge a few feet ahead, then dropped the egg onto the pavement. "Check that out."

A duckling embryo lay exposed within the shattered shell.

Steve went on, "Can you believe they eat those things?"

The crunch of beak and bones, and the texture of intestines and feathers, didn't appeal to me. "Kind of hard," I said. Nobody forced us to eat duck embryos, but if they favored them, who was I to judge? *Weren't we here to help these people? Didn't that include respecting their culture?* Food thrown on the ground wasn't a sign of respect in my mind. And with that, in my eyes Steve and I had become two "ugly Americans," like those I'd read about in school. I worked to suppress my embarrassment over the fact that I was likely an ugly American, too. And another chunk of my notion of American moral purity and superiority crumbled.

I enjoyed a banana on an early foray to the beach across the street from the Two Corps Headquarters. (Omnipresent, it seemed, friendly roving vendors never missed an opportunity to sell fresh fruit or cooked duck eggs.)

BABYSITTER REQUIRED

Steve rushed into the office, back from the mail run. "Hey, guys, we got a newbie, and I heard we're on the moon."

Our vocal office celebration spread with contagion.

I pumped a closed fist. "Yeah." *Our office newbie can wait a few minutes.* "We beat the commie bastards." A mix of images of our race into space over the past decade came to mind, reminding me I no longer followed my space dream, but instead occupied a table in puke-green fatigues on a much different path. I'd dreamed of going into space two-and-a-half years earlier, and thought I knew how to get there. I'd do undergraduate engineering school and campus air force ROTC at U of L. Then, I'd get a Master's in aeronautical engineering as an air force pilot and work my way into our astronaut corps. But my dream collapsed when I developed myopia, which required eyeglasses. I knew the air force had a strict rule requiring pilots and astronauts to have perfect vision, so I'd given up that dream and soured on the military. It had never occurred to me that my space dream had required I be a lifer in the air force!

Amidst our excitement, John took over the introductions for our office cherry. "Listen up. Say hello to Paul, everyone. Help him get settled in."

An opportunity to stretch my legs, I approached Paul and offered my hand. "Welcome. Where're you from?"

"Connecticut," he said with a smile. He appeared deliberate and calm. Pale-skinned, a little puffy in the face.

Not enough outdoor time? I noticed his right eyelid twitch behind his army glasses.

"You?" he added.

"Kentucky," I said. He seemed a likable guy, but I tested the water. "Hey, man, you saw the beach out front? You play football or Frisbee?"

"Yeah."

"We'll go for a workout soon."

In-country for three weeks, long enough to submerge into the daily routine, I missed Rudy's camaraderie. Before he shipped home, I'd spent most every minute of office time with him, and his absence left me a little lonelier, but I stood a little closer to the end of my three-sixty-five, too, when I'd catch my own "freedom bird" back to "the World"—if I didn't get zipped into a plastic bag.

Click! Static, chopped music and voices made it obvious John was searching through the frequencies on our office radio. We briefly listened in on Armed Forces Radio now and then. Most of our news from "the World" arrived in our mail and in *Newsweek* and *Time*, both magazines easy to get. As our access to television in English was extremely limited, we passed along tidbits of news like school-girl gossip.

Raines didn't want the radio on most of the time. Brass had banned music in the workplace, and with a gaggle of officers right outside our door, one could walk in unannounced if they wanted.

"You're listening to Armed Forces Radio," the announcer's voice said. "Here's the latest news. The United States has landed men on the moon. ..."

Everyone in the office got quiet for the replay of Armstrong's words when he'd stepped off the lander: "One small step ... ."

A few minutes later, John switched off the radio. "That's enough," he said.

Neil Armstrong went to the moon … and I went to 'Nam.

* * *

At the end of our workday, John said, "Your turn for babysitter duty, Hogan. Follow me." A few steps outside our office, he pointed. "I want you to wait here during your duty. If the general requests any information, you're here to respond."

"Respond to what, Sarge?"

"Steve will stay and explain the drill."

I grabbed the closest empty chair at the desk by the office-suite entrance, posted at the pleasure of the general. *At least this glorified guard duty doesn't involve a weapon.*

"It's you and me, bud," Steve said. He grabbed the chair at the adjacent desk. "I'll hang back and give you the skinny."

Our other office mates filed out and headed down the hallway, followed by Lieutenant Raines. Last out, John switched off the fans and lights in our office.

Steve didn't break a sweat, appearing to be an old hand at navigating the ins and outs of babysitting. "Get comfortable."

"Sure thing, Steve," I said, though not sure at all—my derrière planted in the hot seat and subject to the whim of the general, Corps Commander. There was nobody with more authority over my life in 'Nam than that guy, unless you considered the head honcho at MACV in Saigon.

"You need to remain here in case the general wants information. Wait to get the 'all clear' before you leave. Okay?"

"Yeah," I said. *What other choice do I have?*

"Most of the time, you won't need to do anything."

"Most?"

"As in probably not," Steve said.

"What would the general want?"

"Most likely a report that's been filed away."

"A filed report?" I asked.

"Yeah. That's as clear as mud, ain't it?"

I imagined myself under pressure, fumbling around to find and present a piece of paper that the general deemed significant.

Officers trickled out from their work area and left the suite. The day's busyness faded, and the office suite and hallway were quieter by the minute as echoes died away.

"May as well turn off the overhead lights," Steve said and nodded. "Catch that switch behind you."

Softer shadows of light through the nearby windows replaced the overhead fluorescent glare and my sense of interrogation. I noticed the absence of an overhead fan. The high humidity and warm temperature pushed my body, cooped up in fatigues, toward an act of perspiration.

"Oh, don't forget." Steve leaned in my direction. "Keep our office radio off. The 'old man' doesn't want music in the Hotel. No unwholesome music" with a heavy emphasis "touting drugs, sex, and rock 'n' roll allowed in the workplace." He grinned.

"I got the drift. Loud and clear. Nothing to encourage goofing off. Everyone crisp, neat, tidy, and anal. Army brass loves anal."

"Say, I need to take a leak." Steve rose from his seat. "Hold the fort. I'll be back in a minute."

"I ain't going anywhere." Wouldn't dare; John's "marching orders" made clear to me.

With the usual noise of conversations, shuffled papers, and chairs pushed and pulled across the linoleum floor absent in the office suite, I heard Steve's footsteps reverberate down the hallway, then stairwell, as they faded into silence.

I wondered if the "old guy," the Corps general, commanding, would request information before Steve returned. *Hurry up and wait.*

With the room darkened, I felt entombed. And the air was so still, I imagined I could hear dust settling. No books or magazines in sight. Death from a bullet or grenade didn't appeal, but a demise from boredom held no appeal either and, to boot, would draw out the agony. I wouldn't have dared bring a cassette player or porn mag to the office. If the general discovered me with nude photos in the building, I'd be cornered with little recourse. *Would the general care to look at some porn, Sir?*

The desk drawers called to me.

In a haphazard search, I rifled through the untidy loose paper clips, rubber bands, notepads, pens, and pencils in the middle drawer. Not inclined to rearrange anything—more a cursory shopper—I moved on to explore elsewhere. The Hotel's hard flooring amplified footsteps, a warning from the hallway.

Motionless, I held my breath. My chair's location prevented the discovery of a finger up my nose or my feet on the desk by quiet, prying eyes from down the hall.

A door opened, then closed.

I leaned to the side for a peek out of the suite and down the hallway to the CO's office. *Phew. Whoever it was headed into the general's office. All quiet on the northern front.*

I tugged at another drawer. *Locked. Not for my eyes.*

A third drawer opened. Empty folders and plain paper intermingled in a heap. One hand deep into the pile, I seized a pocket dictionary as an object of immediate interest, leaned back in the chair, propped my feet on the desk, and thumbed a few pages. *Any page will do.* I ran my index finger down the page for a word to catch my eye.

Extant. Hmm, a new word to me. Started reading in a whisper, "Latin origin; not extinct." *Yeah, as opposed to dead. Good word. Used in a sentence—I'm extant, not extinct.*

I flipped through several pages.

"Fickle: changeable; capricious." *Used in a sentence—Life is fickle, it's extant one minute, extinct the next.*

I thumbed more pages.

"Subsist: to remain alive." *Another good word. I subsist, therefore I'm not extinct.*

Footsteps echoed up the stairwell. The sound growing louder, I leaned from my perch and watched Steve walk up.

"And I'm back," he said.

"I thought you'd gone extinct. Everything come out all right?"

"Yeah, nothing exciting, a little of this, a little of that. Gen-gen didn't want to party?"

"No, I'm thankful to say."

"Never requested information from me. His aide will notify you when you're no longer needed."

"The sooner, the better," I said.

Steve checked his watch. "Shouldn't be too much longer. I haven't stayed more than a couple of hours. You're probably good for the rest of your shift. Anyway, I'm getting thirsty. Time for a little grub before I head to the Enlisted Men's Club for a drink. Join me there?"

"If I don't melt into this chair."

Alone again, I sat stuck with nothing to do except wait. Wait for the general to do or not to do. Wait at a desk where I didn't want to sit for a potential request I never wanted to hear. Time squandered.

The more I thought, the hotter I burned. Hurry up and wait, always the army's way of doing things—always started with a great sense of urgency, followed by a lot of time wasted doing little or nothing.

Tired of getting jerked around, dumped on, and unappreciated, I imagined that most Americans back in the States and not subject to the draft considered themselves unaffected by the war and went through their days disconnected and oblivious to 'Nam, like I had, considering 'Nam a mere periodic, inconvenient interruption in their personal lives. I'd watched people my age and younger on TV yelling, holding signs that portrayed the war as a misguided shit-pile venture, and calling 'Nam vets traitors and baby-killers. I didn't see myself as a baby-killer, but maybe those protesters had a point. My anger grew, oozed from every pore, and mixed with the sweat under my fatigues over my notion that the draft process, though following guidelines, felt arbitrary and capricious, as it weighed more heavily on those who couldn't afford or get into college. Beyond that, Nixon, Congress, and the draft board people weren't the ones in danger. We Americans weren't sharing that burden equally. *They can all go to hell!*

Too late to change the fact that the army had glued my butt firmly to a chair in 'Nam. But I fixed my mind on my payback if I returned to "the World" in one piece. If I could keep my shit together and leave the army with an honorable discharge, I'd extract every cent I could from Uncle Sam through the GI Bill. That, at least in a small way, would avenge my year's exile to 'Nam. Moreover, without a dream to replace becoming an engineer and astronaut, aside from furthering my relationship with Pam, I felt detached from any future, and needed every anchor to home to which I could cling. I wanted to avoid being mentally swallowed up by my shit-situation and I'd need more than the distractions of booze and nudie magazines.

Pam's next letter? Nothing to do except wait and wonder about her next letter and the general's notions. Perhaps, a shit-storm flurry of activity would erupt, generated by a wild hair sprouted from the CO's ass. *Best to distract myself.*

"Boredom: uninterested; ennui." *Ooh, fancy word, ennui.*

"Ennui: French origin, weariness and dissatisfaction." *Good word. I wallow in a state of ennui. Bored out of my fucking gourd, I could die from ennui within days ... weeks, my will to live sucked out of me by army regimentation if I don't fight back.*

A slight breeze pushed through the open window nearby. *Nice.* I glanced at my watch. *Shit, another thirty-five minutes, according to Steve.*

Sporadic faint noises through the hallway proved there were other people in the building. *Corps CO in his office?* Be damned, I wouldn't knock on his door to find out.

"Cavorting: to leap about; prance; to romp about happily; frolic." *Yeah, that fits. If I weren't stuck babysitting, I'd be cavorting or romping on the beach ... or drinking.*

Not sure what the CO might want, I could explain the meaning of ennui or cavorting to him. With another glance at my watch, I expected I'd leave within a few minutes unless the general caught a second wind.

An office door opened and footsteps grew louder. I peeked around the corner.

A khaki-uniformed corporal approached within ten feet. "All clear. You may leave now."

I nodded. "Thanks."

Without hesitation, I shoved the dictionary back into its drawer, and doubled-timed to hunt down Steve.

* * *

"What took you so long?" Steve asked.

"You know me, stayed and watched the paint dry," I told him. "Double vodka orange," I told the waiter.

While I sucked down my first doses of medicinal alcohol from a disposable cup, I pondered my life at Two Corps Command.

Who knew how many demerits I'd avoided while being deprived of cavorting and frolicking during my babysitting? Who knew how many karma brownie points I'd earned? From my perspective, that had been a total waste, except for my dictionary study. Those lazy, ungrateful fuckers back in "the World" would pay for me to go back to college with their tax dollars ... if I survived 'Nam.

PLAYING HOUSE

The next day, Saturday and in the office, Elliot pulled Paul, Steve, and me aside. Self-assured, he said, "Come over to my place tonight and meet my old lady."

Living off base against army policy? He'd said it as if an overnight hangout among the locals was obvious and natural—as easy as I'd say, Water is wet. *A little cocky, but we'll get along if you don't lord anything over me.*

"Anh wants me to marry her and take her to the States, but I'm not going to," he said. "I've got a fiancée back home in New York."

Fiancée? You're a real shit. What kind of way is that to treat a girl? I couldn't see myself doing that, but I figured having an apartment in Nha Trang and two-timing his "old lady" back in New York was his business, so I kept my mouth shut.

Since Rudy left, I'd stayed current on my incoming reports and updated my wall map with little black symbols. Better yet, I'd faced no pestering requests from Gaston. I expected he'd lay an order on me eventually, but I felt no inclination to hurry one along.

After each day's work, though immersed in my daily personal activities and out of the immediate presence of uniformed lifers, reminders of my presence in 'Nam remained unavoidable. And that reality gnawed on me like a starved dog working over a bone. As an escape and to distract myself, I considered engaging in any activity that didn't strike me as outright stupid.

I nodded to Elliot. "Yeah, sure."

✳ ✳ ✳

Elliot placed his hand on her shoulder. "This is Anh."

Petite, short, in her early twenties, her smile displayed a crooked front tooth.

Pretty, despite that tooth.

Anh turned to another woman, who'd appeared at her side. "This is Ming, my sister."

Take Anh, add five years, a few pounds, some wrinkles, a broader nose … and voilà: Ming. Didn't appeal to me. She lived with Anh and Elliot, I guessed. I didn't ask, they didn't say. Ming eyed me with a grin.

An unexplainable, kind-of-creepy feeling came over me. *On the hunt for a live-in husband, too?* Bob Dylan performed in my head, "It ain't me, babe … no, no, no … ."

Proud and eager, Anh showed us their apartment. From the building's hallway, we looked through the door at their bedroom, a furnished private living space with a bed, couch, chair, chest of drawers, and built-in closet. Tight, plain, and simple.

Anh led us a few paces down the hallway into a covered courtyard. "I cook here. Everyone in building cook here." Heavy smells of burnt wood and cooked fish with hints of vinegar filled the air.

Pretty good English.

Anh continued, "There is toilet." She pointed toward a bare light bulb, turned off, which dangled by its electrical cord over a squat-toilet hole in the ground.

I didn't dare go any nearer that scaled-down version of Camp Shit-Burn. "Elliot, do you coach her?" I asked. "I mean with her English."

"Yeah, she's eager to learn," he said.

We retraced our steps down the hallway.

Anh opened a different door, climbed a few steps, looked back, and with a motion said, "Come. This is second bedroom."

The double-sized bed, pushed against one wall, accentuated the no-frills accommodation. Simple, clean—an enviable bedroom by Vietnamese standards, I figured. An improvement over a dirt-floor thatched hooch in the jungle occupied by mosquitoes.

Elliot explained, "I give Anh money to run the house, and I stay here overnight as often as possible."

Most of the time, no doubt.

We retreated into the downstairs bedroom. Ming took the chair. Elliot offered Steve, Paul, and me the couch and I grabbed the position farthest from Ming.

I studied a framed picture of an older couple on one wall. *Had to be Anh's and Ming's parents.*

Anh clung to Elliot's arm as they sat side by side on the bed.

I recalled what Elliot had said about not marrying Anh. *Does she even have a clue? How much pain will that inflict on her? She doesn't deserve that kind of treatment.*

Elliot pulled out a baggie. "Want to smoke some dope?"

"Is the earth round?" Steve asked.

Paul nodded. "Yeah."

"Why not?" I added.

Encouraged by his three guests, Elliot rolled a joint, lit it, took a drag, then passed it on.

Steve offered it to me with a "Here you go, dude."

This was my debut with the free-love generation's equivalent of alcohol rolled in cigarette paper. *What's the harm? I know these guys. We're safe, enclosed in Elliot's apartment. Probably safe. Most likely safe. Elliot lives here and he's still alive.*

I inhaled my first drag, long and deep. I knew how, I'd seen that in movies. *Cough!* A sense of ease, well-being, and contentment washed over me like warm Kentucky rain.

Primed to get high, set for launch, and prepared for my weightlessness as a helium-filled balloon, I studied the ceiling. I imagined myself floating there. *The ceiling will stop me. Prevent my floating away, won't it? Probably will … and if the door is closed, I'll stay in the apartment.*

My reverie broken by a change in the conversation, a shift of inflection on a word, or one thought rooted in reality that had bubbled up from the depths of my brain—I didn't know what—I glanced down. Both of my arms and one leg suspended in midair, I held a contorted horizontal karate pose.

I eased down onto the couch. *Had anyone noticed?* They were busy conversing. For me, getting high was no longer a rumor or a myth created by Hollywood. Aware of Ming again, I renewed my vigilance, prepared to fend off any physical advances. She looked hungry for a man.

Anh whispered something in Elliot's ear.

He looked our way. "Time for bed. It's past curfew, too late to get back to the Compound. You guys can spend the night upstairs."

Paul and Steve, closer to the door, headed out ahead of me.

Elliot offered me the baggie of remaining weed, along with rolling papers. "Here, take the rest of this ganja."

I grabbed the stash and got the hell out of there before Ming attached herself to me. I figured she'd sleep on the couch, but that wasn't my concern.

The upstairs bed was only large enough for two, and since I had no interest in occupying the middle of a three-man sandwich, I parked in the stairwell with the dope and cigarette papers.

Any way to get higher?

"Where did Connard go?" Steve asked Paul.

"I don't know," Paul answered.

Quiet, like a kid who'd sneaked cookies, I huffed and puffed on my treasure until the stash was exhausted. I didn't feel any higher. But then again, I was probably already too stoned to know the difference.

When I finally climbed the stairs, I discovered Steve and Paul were out cold, breathing heavy and snoring with their arms and legs dangling off the bed. With no bed cover and no pillow, I befriended the bare wood floor and, half-dazed, waited for the hours to pass.

Sometime after daybreak, Steve, Paul, and I hustled back to the Compound.

I re-entered the Compound tired and with a dishrag mouth, no longer a cannabis virgin. But until I was under the direct eye of "the man" on Monday, and with no need to report for work on Sunday, I could lay low after I'd gotten some chow.

EATING APPLES

Late Monday morning, Steve set a brown paper-wrapped parcel on my work table. "You lucky devil, you got a package," he said.

The date was stamped a mere five days before, from what I made out. "Yeah, a 'care package' from Mom."

Steve eyed me. "Aren't you going to open it?"

"I'll wait till lunch break." In-country about two months, I savored my mail, an umbilical cord to "the World."

* * *

On my bunk, alone in the barrack, I worked my way into the box, removing wadded newspaper. *Mom's bombproof packaging. Let's see, washcloth, towel, T-shirt, can of salted peanuts, a bar of soap. Yay, a letter.*

I could get by without those things, but each one was good for my soul. The last item still in the box, the largest and a little mashed on one side, lay wrapped in aluminum foil inside a clear plastic bag. *Cake?* Reminded me of the story Mom and Dad had told Verlon and me.

"Always on the move across the Pacific," Dad had explained, "we never knew when the Japanese might attack us, and the navy never told us where we were going. They didn't allow us to tell anyone in our letters where we were."

82

Mom had said with a big grin, "I baked your daddy a cake for his first Christmas away, wrapped it in waxed paper, and put it in a box. Then I wrapped the box in butcher paper. Tied that all up with twine."

Dad continued, "It took three months for that cake to catch up to me. At that point, the box was pretty beat up, but the cake still tasted good."

Both had chuckled.

I'd wondered about the condition of that cake but never questioned Mom or Dad about it, though I must've heard that story a half-dozen times.

The sweet, moist smell of icing, cinnamon, and pecans greeted me as I removed the plastic bag and peeled back the foil.

The barrack screen door slammed. *Clack!*

"Hey, going to share any of that cake?" Steve asked as he pulled up beside me.

"Keep it down, guy. I don't want to give it all away. Get me a knife."

"Okay, between you and me, then." After a short search through his locker, he pulled out an army mess knife—what we called a butter knife at home—and wiped it a couple of times across his shirt.

I gave the knife the once-over, but noticed no obvious dried food on it. *What the hell?*

Steve took a big bite of the piece I handed him. "Mmm, this tastes good."

"Yeah, Mom calls it a Sock-It-To-Me cake, my favorite."

Mom's package reaffirmed that normal life continued at home, which gave me a warm, reassuring sense of well-being about the past and present. Motherhood, apple pie, and the flag—safe.

"You got a birthday coming up?" Steve asked.

"Yeah, twenty-one in a few days."

Adulthood by virtue of age felt unfitting and hollow to me, a booby prize of sorts. No matter that others considered me an adult until I did. I'd yet to discover the answer to the other big question that consumed my teen years: What would make me a grown-up?

Vote? I'd ruled that out as a gauge. After the fact, my first vote for Nixon for his second presidential term had seemed unwise, though he had promised to get us out of Vietnam. Lots of people had voted for him and a lot of people seemed pretty stupid to me, so I figured some had closed their eyes or held their noses and pinned the tail on the donkey. Either way, they hadn't done any worse than me.

Drive? I got my license at eighteen, a big deal at the time. I wondered about the comments from fellow senior students in high school who'd boasted about accidents they'd caused. Got mine out of the way, they'd joked, as if their accidents were a curse every driver was destined to experience at least once. I wondered if and when I'd get into an accident, too; adulthood did not seem to be required.

Smoke? When a runt, I'd puffed on cigarettes around several older cousins, though hadn't inhaled. I imagined myself a big shot, but "smoking" hadn't changed my thinking about anything, though I wondered if the adult warnings were true that tobacco would stunt my growth.

Use drugs? My recent ganja encounter had made no difference as to my perception of achieving manhood, particularly since I hadn't enjoyed free love with a sexy, attractive girl, though I admittedly hadn't conducted a thorough study.

Drink alcohol? I'd tied on a few binges since early teen-hood that led to episodes of uncontrollable staggers and the stupidity of slurred speech before the effects wore off. Hadn't made me more of a man by a long shot, though Dad seemed to offer himself up as a drinking-man role model.

Serve in the military? I'd entered the army ass-first, not by any well-thought-out design. The army wasn't particular from what I'd observed, either, and many nose-pickers had been accepted. A history lesson of General Custer provided me a perfect example of officers with poor judgment making bad decisions—hardly a faultless model of manhood.

Lose my virginity? Maybe that was it. I'd hoped to lose mine since thirteen, but no girl ever gave me the chance. My every other thought was, What the hell was wrong with me? Solo private activities had provided me little satisfaction, nor a clue about the real thing. So, until I experienced sex with a girl, toward which my hormones propelled me, I could only imagine that to be my last hurdle to manhood.

Steve looked at me with his mischievous grin. "You need to celebrate. Let's go to a whorehouse. I know of a few in town."

Going there might make me a target of every VC or NVA who could get me in their gunsight, but I felt driven to take the risk. "Okay, sure." *My virginity problem needs a fix.*

"Let's go tonight."

If not tonight, when?

I'd never tried to find a prostitute back home. Didn't know where to start. Feared one might eat me alive, but I felt prepared to handle one in 'Nam, as long as she didn't pull a bamboo shiv.

* * *

After dinner and showers, Steve and I headed down quiet, potholed streets through residential neighborhoods. A million questions passed by on my mental conveyor belt. But I didn't want Steve to think me a complete idiot, so I kept my lips zipped.

With no streetlights and an overcast sky, darkness provided cover for movement and an opportunity to avoid hostile eyes. After our eyes adjusted, the faint random light from the interiors of surrounding houses allowed our progress without a major pothole-mishap. The crunch of footsteps on the dusty graveled streets from the vague forms that approached and passed by told us we weren't alone in the streets. Other men in fatigues, in ones and twos from the little I saw, no doubt hunted for similar pleasures. The scuffles of feet over gravel beyond what I could make out left me to imagine who made them. *Charlie roaming the streets, too?* The wafting, changing smells of incense offered proof of residents all around us, though unseen and unheard.

Steve pointed. "Let's try this one."

Didn't matter to me which brothel we visited, as long as we didn't end up in a den of VC.

I paid little attention to the house as we climbed the steps to the front door, detecting nothing odd. It was no different from any other house around, except for the meager red glow cast by a weak bulb.

An older woman, the madam, no doubt, ushered us from the door to a couch. "Sit, please." Two large indents in the padded couch, pale spots of worn crimson velvet, suggested where to plant our asses.

Everything was long past new and in need of repair. A prominent staircase with a heavy wooden railing led to a second floor, and the dark, flowery wallpaper hinted at cathouses I'd seen in Westerns. The thick smell of burnt sandalwood that lodged in my nose suggested otherwise.

Within the minute, two females about our ages presented themselves and took seats in front of us.

"Which one stirs your coffee?" Steve asked.

"Doesn't matter. Both look good to me."

"I'll take the one on the right," he said.

As if there was no time to waste, Steve negotiated terms with that girl and disappeared up the stairs.

I feasted on the sight of the remaining young woman, who remained quiet. Long, straight dark hair hung past her shoulders. Braless, her nipples announced themselves through a skimpy halter top. The top's low V-cut exposed delicate, well-shaped breasts that formed a perfect cleavage and enticed me to touch the little of what remained hidden from my view. Her miniskirt invited a sneak preview, but she kept her legs together. That and the dim lighting suggested she'd get paid before I saw those lady parts.

I'd explore her in a New York minute … touch every inch, wallow in my excitement and pleasure, and discover sex, but I froze. *Is she an innocent fawn in the brush or a cat on the prowl? Does that even matter? Why am I hesitating?*

Mom's warning came to mind: Don't let a young girl ruin you. Her words mingled with and stepped all over my vision of heated rabbit sex.

What the hell?

Mom never said much more during the times she had "that talk" with me. I knew she'd meant that I shouldn't get a girl pregnant and be forced into a marriage. I'd wanted to slink away and avoid the topic at all cost. Figured silent attentiveness to be a better strategy and least apt to prolong the conversation. Dad, on the other hand, a vacuum of information, never once offered a discussion or invited questions.

For years, highlighted by a morning erection, my lust, the same as sleep and hunger, started each day with a simple goal and grew into an obsession until attended to. Now, I wasn't sure how I needed to get from my place of inhibition to a physical free-flow of instinct. In awkward silence, I stared into her dark-brown eyes. She stared back.

What is she thinking? Probably that I was an idiot. I was.

About fifteen minutes later, Steve reappeared. "Well, did you?"

"No."

"All right, no problem, let's go." Didn't raise his voice or give me the stink-eye.

We headed back toward the Compound. The residential streets remained dark and quiet.

Damn, why hadn't I done it? If not now, when? No reason why I shouldn't; I didn't need to worry about getting her pregnant. Time for me to taste the forbidden fruit. "Fuck it, Steve, I'm going for it. Let's score some dope."

"Okay," he said, "I know a place."

* * *

A few blocks on, Steve provided a one-handed motion toward a corner house with the lights on. "Here we go, one-stop shopping."

A heavy smell of musk and burnt wood greeted us near the open front door, a pleasant fragrance after I surrendered and inhaled deeply.

Steve knocked.

A weathered, dark-haired woman beckoned us in. The madam, no doubt. Soft lights illuminated a calm and quiet interior, with no hustle and bustle or young women pushing drinks. Several fingers of smoke curled from incense sticks on a small table.

After a couple of words in Pidgin English and the universal sign for smoking from Steve, she caught his drift and produced a joint.

Steve pulled out some military script. "I'll cover this one." He produced his Bic and lit the thin joint with a long pull. He paused a moment, then offered it to me with an exhale, "Your highway to heaven."

With a deep inhale, I waited for the effect. A peaceful sensation washed through me. *Yeah.* "Down to business, Steve."

"You'll need to negotiate the price with her," he said.

I looked at the madam, motioned with my hands, and said, "How much?"

A mouthful of ebony teeth greeted me when she grinned, my first real look at her up close in the dim light. *Good God.*

Pressing matter at hand and in no mood to get sidetracked, I gave her the asking price, which seemed reasonable to me. Not sure what to expect, I figured she'd summon girls from a hidden place for me to make a final choice. Instead, she motioned me to follow, led me into the adjacent bedroom, removed her clothing without hesitation, and waited on the bed with a big grin.

There I stood, about to get personal with black teeth, wrinkled skin, and flat, sagging boobs. *Jesus, how old is she?* Didn't matter. I'd have humped any female with a pulse right then. Determined, I beat down every excuse to back out. *No need to give her the tongue … or even kiss her. That's not the part of her that interests me, anyway.*

I chanted to myself as I removed my fatigues, *Focus.*

Stripped, I lay on top of her. *Focus.*

The feel of her body heat and soft breasts against my chest shocked me. I hadn't expected to feel her body warmth on my skin. Then again, I didn't really know what to expect.

She took a firm grasp of me, then guided me in for my first push, my discovery of first sex. Wet and warm. I hadn't expected either of those.

Oh, yes.

And, just like that, no longer a virgin, I considered my curse broken. As we continued, a dark gloom lifted. I felt no shame or embarrassment, just gratitude. Her gentle smile soothed and comforted me, despite her darkened enamel.

As my head eased close to her shoulder, I noticed a faint, delicate fragrance of flowers mixed with sweat. *Ah, the smell of a woman.*

I wasted no time. Wanted to explode inside her. Wanted to discover the answer to the question I'd obsessed over during the past seven years: What's all the hoo-ha over sex?

And when I came inside her, that boatload of tortured ideas and unending questions during my decade of teen-hood melted away. End of question. I considered myself a man at last.

A breath or two afterward, I rolled off of her. Still wet and hard, I gave her a nod and smiled as I pulled on my clothes.

She smiled in silence.

A few steps out of the bedroom, I gave Steve a big grin. "Happy birthday to me."

We hustled back to the Compound.

It didn't occur to me then that my determination to reach manhood had been arbitrarily based on a sex act and that manhood, or for that matter adulthood, should be based upon the development of emotional balance and maturity, which I certainly didn't possess. Dad's episodes of drunken-rages, and reluctance to otherwise share of himself, hadn't provided a healthy model of how I should express myself. I couldn't see that the choice of utilizing prostitutes would allow me to limp along without the necessity of openly sharing feelings of intimacy—something that would take me years to develop.

* * *

Before work the next morning, Steve pulled up by me at our latrine urinal trough.

"How's it hanging?" Steve asked.

I paused a moment. "I'm getting a burning sensation when I piss."

He laughed. "Ooh, you need to go on sick call."

* * *

The following day after work, Steve claimed a shower sprinkler head near mine in the otherwise empty latrine, and asked me, "Say, how's that problem?"

"Much better. The doc gave me meds."

"Get a lecture, too?" he asked.

"No. The doc was cool."

Steve paused, then flashed a sheepish grin. "I'm getting a burning sensation when I piss."

I laughed. "Ooh, you need to go on sick call, too."

* * *

"Ready for town again?" Steve asked me a couple of days later.

"Yeah, Steve. Got your problem taken care of, have you?"

"Cleared right up."

My head hair—the little of it not cropped away by eager barbers—had been organized by a comb, and I was plastered in Old Spice aftershave and deodorant. We hustled past the guard at the gate. Going together fit my way of thinking, a wingman buddy system for safety. And with my virginity issue resolved, I defined sex as ongoing recreation, regardless of VD.

Steve looked up the street. "Let's catch a ride." He spotted one coming from the other way and said, "There's one." He gave the driver a wave.

The Vietnamese taxi, a three-wheeled minivan, screeched to a stop.

"We call these things Lambrettas," Steve said.

The rig's tailgate had been removed, so Steve and I easily climbed into the canvas-covered passenger area in the back. Sole riders, we claimed spots on long, wooden benches opposite each other and staggered ourselves to avoid banging knees.

"Hue Street," Steve instructed the driver through the open sliding window between us and the driver's seat.

The guy nodded, slipped the transmission into gear, then revved the engine. Vibrations from the overgrown eggbeater massaged my ass while our driver's taxi jostled us about, though he slowed and weaved through the streets using motorcycle-style handlebars to avoid the deepest potholes.

I hunched forward and twisted sideways for views out the sides. *Hell … we were sitting ducks. Any joker on a motorbike with a pistol could shoot us.*

I glanced at the driver, then through his dusty windshield. "Keep this rig rolling, dude," I mumbled. Knew he wouldn't understand my words, even if he'd heard them.

Steve leaned forward. "Hey, here's an idea. Let's jump out."

What? We both had the money for the ride, I knew, but I didn't want Steve to think me a wimp. "Okay," I said.

"Wait till we slow down. I'll give you the word."

I nodded in recognition.

The driver prepared to negotiate a busy intersection and a cloud of street dust engulfed us from behind.

I waved my hand and tasted grit. *Ptui!*

Steve made a move. "Go," he yelled.

We scrambled out and ran across the intersection while the driver yelled in incomprehensible syllables.

I didn't look back.

When Steve and I stopped running, we shared a good laugh, but my guilt and shame made it clear to me that I'd been an ugly American. And yet another chunk of the notion of my individual American moral purity and superiority crumbled.

A few blocks' walk brought us to the nightclubs, clustered together in the street-lit part of town. People on foot and motorbikes clogged the streets in a noisy moving mass, which reminded me of a state fair midway. No doubt, to me it offered some small escape from reality for those who came to recreate. Provided a steady income for those who worked in the shops, bars, and restaurants. Offered the chance of survival for some who pushed carts and carried their wares on poles through the streets as they eked out a few bowls of rice.

We bobbed and weaved through the swarm of people on our way down the street, and although a head taller than most of those around me, I felt less conspicuous, less vulnerable to Charlie.

"Keep a tight grip on your wallet," Steve said. "A gang of three-foot pickpockets attacked me around here once."

Immersed in a cesspool of who-knows-what criminal behavior, everybody appeared on the hustle. In a different kind of warfare than in the jungle, I guarded against an unidentified enemy of grifters and pint-sized thieves plying their skills.

The smell of sandalwood and sounds of Jimi Hendrix's "Purple Haze" poured into the street as a nightclub barker beckoned, "Come in, GI."

Steve and I entered and assessed the joint for threats, the music loud and out of place. Wisps of incense smoke curled from scattered locations on tables and the bar counter, serving as distractions from the whiff of stench. *Mold? Dead rat in a wall? Refuse ditch out the open back door?* I considered all of those to be distinct possibilities.

Not much difference between the smells and life in the cities and jungles of 'Nam, I figured. Incense couldn't hide the reek that filled many of the streets—not for me, anyway. Impossible to disguise the odor of a buffalo patty, even when drenched in French perfume.

A sprinkle of GIs seated at tables, drinks in hand, chatted with females in plumage.

Bar girls, every one.

One fellow sat alone, clad in fatigues similar to ours, though obviously a member of the army of South Vietnam, Republic of. Little to no spare money to attract bargirl attention, I concluded. Those guys didn't get paid much, from what I'd learned.

"You numba one, GI. You like, GI? You buy me drink?" a flaming-redheaded mini-skirted girl asked.

It was a wig, no question. She wanted people to notice her. Hard at work, she wasted no time in her effort to separate my money from me. "No," I told her.

"Well, what do you think?" Steve asked.

"Give me another minute and I'll report my findings."

Though I'd had an inglorious beginning, I wanted to retain a respectable minimum standard regarding who I'd sleep with, as if I could be choosy under the circumstance. I hoped I'd learned something from my initial dose of the clap, though it sure as hell wasn't abstinence. I ran through my basic checklist as I scanned the few young females in sight. *Breasts? Hair? Arms and legs? Teeth?*

Though hard to tell if all their parts were real, those indigenous females measured up to my initial scrutiny, at least to warrant a sustained look. None, however, stirred me enough to overcome my unease and lack of confidence in talking my way into their panties … if they wore any. I figured I'd need to talk a "damn good game" to overcome the odds that they would give anything away for free.

Steve moved toward the bar and said, "In the meantime, let's get a drink."

Positioned next to Steve on a stool, I asked the bartender for a rum and Coke, and after a moment's pause, added, "No ice." I turned to Steve, and though I figured I preached to the choir, said, "Don't trust the ice. At least rum and Coke come from a bottle."

Steve nodded to the bartender. "Same-same," he said, then asked me, "See anybody here you're interested in?"

Ready to get laid again, but without a reasonable prospect, other than paying for a prostitute, I said, "No need to spend money on drinks here." *God, what I wouldn't give to lay Pam.* "Besides, I need to keep a steady eye on my monthly pay. I've decided to save up for new wheels back home. Gave my car to my brother when I left and don't consider it right to ask him to return it."

"Still willing to spend money on hookers, though?" Steve quipped.

"Well … some sacrifices are called for."

Steve chuckled, then tossed back his drink in long gulps. "Let's go, then," he said, and placed his empty glass on the bar.

We fell back to plan B and headed to the dark-street red-light part of town.

* * *

"Come in, GI," a young female beckoned in a cheery voice.

The driving beat of Credence Clearwater Revival and the sweet-flowery fragrance of burning incense had acted as homing beacons the last few yards to this makeshift lounge. It helped grease my wheels, though I needed no additional lubrication.

Steve told the girl behind the makeshift bar, "Beer."

I waggled two fingers and made sure she understood that I wanted one as well.

Our beers bought us time to study the goods and further blunted my constant edge of tension.

Several GIs with beers chatted up girls one-on-one.

Why the hell spend money on them to talk?

Two girls not otherwise occupied made a beeline toward Steve and me after they secured eye contact. Already stiff, the dim lighting and my male hormones encouraged my imagination to improve upon their facial features. They approached us as if they'd already decided which one of us they'd fuck—as if Steve and I didn't have any say in the matter. I sucked down the remainder of my suds.

As the one who approached me drew near, I caught a whiff of perfume, faint but distinct and pleasing. She was a near-perfect specimen of femaleness with a soft, smooth face, erect breasts that pointed the way, and shoulder-length straight black hair combed. She smiled.

No discussion. Steve and I looked at each other, nodded, and headed out of the lounge on our separate explorations.

I felt my quiet, dark-eyed companion's hand eagerly search for mine as we crossed the dimly lit street. With each step, my anticipation grew with equal measures of excitement and apprehension. My prick discouraged distracting notions. However, though unlikely, I couldn't dismiss the nagging possibility that Charlie may have done the same earlier in the evening or the night before with her … or that a VC hid in the shadows, waiting to cut my throat. If nothing else, I felt suspicious because everything had seemed all too easy.

My partner-in-fornication (I hoped) indicated with a gentle motion of her hand and a lean against me to head through an open front door lit by soft, white light into a neighborhood house. Straightaway we entered a cubicle not much larger than the bed inside, with stark bare walls, no mosquito net, a small side table, and a blanket for a door.

Basic, but better than a dirt-floor hooch in the jungle.

Straight to business, she removed her clothes, lay down on the bed, waited, and watched me.

I tried to present an air of nonchalance, though I pulled off my fatigues in a hurry, fearing I'd cream my pants as I feasted on her naked body. I was delayed momentarily, however, when my shorts hung up on my full erection.

How different she is from my first! Closer to my age and with white teeth, she rivaled my image of a *Playboy* centerfold, only she was indigenous.

She accommodated me as I felt my way into her. We gazed into each other's eyes, our bodies pressed against each other. The touch of her firm breasts and hard nipples, and her heavy breath, further excited me.

Oh, yes. No longer alone, I've returned to that primordial sanctuary of body and soul.

Since my last encounter, I'd missed that physical closeness, reminded by her body heat, her rhythm of breath and pulse, all separate from my sensations of penetration. I'd missed the closeness of a lingering hug from another human being, not a fleeting slap on the back between young men, driven by male taboos and fear of sexual monkey business.

Her smooth skin, unblemished, showed no wrinkles, not a hint. *Jesus, how old is she?* I didn't need to know, though had no difficulty imagining her to be seventeen ... or even sixteen.

Her tenderness and the way she gazed into my eyes, made me forget for those fleeting moments, that we were engaged in a business transaction. Instead, I related to her as a feeling human, which left me to imagine that our encounter was a more loving experience and that she combined the essence of femininity with the purity of love. At that point, I longed to get off the 'Nam merry-go-round, escape from all my inner turmoil, and melt into her and never return.

I exploded inside her, kissed her lips, wanting her to experience all of her female sexual pleasure before we parted, wondering if she had.

If only every sexual encounter could be this tender, and make me feel this connection and oneness. It made me wonder if what I was feeling was love. I could only guess, since my sexual encounters to date could never be confused with anything but the transactional relationships they were.

On our walk back to the lounge, I told her, "You numba one." I knew she understood I meant "You're the best." All the indigenous knew and used that term.

How many soldiers, I wonder now, thought sex with a sweet and tender young prostitute was an expression of love, equally shared by both? I have little doubt, as I look back, that what drove her into my arms was likely much more about survival than a longing for love. And even if she had felt something, whatever tenderness that young girl displayed to me could or would be extinguished within her as she continued on as a prostitute.

* * *

When I walked up, Steve, in the lounge with a bottle of beer in hand, appeared pleased with himself as he sang along to the music, "Born to be wiiiiild."

I motioned to the girl bartender. "Beer."

"Well, grow any oats?" Steve asked, then took a swig of his suds.

"Did my damnedest. Can't believe how young she looked." Didn't want to get into details. "You?" I took a swallow of my beer.

"Best thing since cookies and milk," Steve said.

"I'll be back to visit her again in a few days," I said.

"Good luck," Steve replied. "I've never seen the same one twice. They get moved around as part of the sex trade, I think." He emptied his bottle. "Let's go."

"Sex trade? That hadn't occurred to me." I downed the remains from my bottle. "At least we're helping the local economy," I added as a half-assed joke. But it was a cover for how I felt about that young girl being used in that way. Still I knew I couldn't help those prostitutes one bit. Right or wrong, they were doing their best to survive the 'Nam shit-situation, too.

"Hey, Steve, do you ever wonder what will happen to them after we leave and this war ends? It's got to end sometime."

"I don't think about it much. I suspect most of them will blend in if they survive."

"I hope they can."

BUDDHA

On the bridge, I told the Lambretta driver, "Stop here." Then, I turned to Paul, and said, "Let's walk the rest of the way."

My guard lowered after trips into town with Steve, I ventured out with other buddies. And with no hostile action reported in or around Nha Trang for some months, the sunny Sunday afternoon had encouraged my excursion with Paul.

I'd taken in the scene as we rode north through the crooked streets of Nha Trang toward the Cai River. The lush trees and brilliant flowers, the dark-green covered inland mountains, and the cotton clouds that moved towards a restful sea, belied the nature of the combat zone I inhabited.

"Great bridge, wide lanes, the color of new cement," I told Paul. I glanced around as we leaned on the shiny aluminum railing to survey the Cai below. "I wonder how long it will take Charlie to blow it."

"That would be unpopular with the locals."

I tapped the railing a couple of times with my knuckles. "We must've spent beaucoup bucks to build this."

"A drop in the bucket of what we spend in 'Nam every day."

Numerous huts, built on stilts, crowded together along the river bank. Sampans jostled and parted the floating garbage as they plied up and down the river, everyone busy surviving.

The wind shifted and carried the faint, sour smell of garbage.

"No space wasted … but the sight of all the trash is disgusting. Mom always kept our house clean, at least, and I mowed our lawn every week or two."

"Yeah, but it's the least of their worries," Paul said.

Within view and a short distance away by foot, the white Buddha statue beckoned.

I turned. "Let's go."

On the highest hill around town, Buddha waited, sitting crossed-legged in a lotus blossom, forty feet from head to seat. A plaque at the base informed me, "… second largest Buddha … largest in Korea."

My short-lived reflection on Buddha's serenity evaporated when thoughts of a barrack-mate's former description of Tet fighting crowded in. "… heavy fighting … on the north end of Nha Trang across the river around the big Buddha statue." I scanned the surroundings, peaceful at the moment.

Reminded that death lurked everywhere and visited some unlucky GIs across 'Nam every day, I re-examined the statue of Buddha, eyes closed in meditation, indifferent to the human suffering around us. Squalor, filth, and death in the midst of sublime beauty—that was the nature of 'Nam.

North of the Cai River and downtown Nha Trang, I posed at the
prominent white Buddha statue. (A fixed plaque indicated a taller
version was in South Korea.)

BREAK A LEG

"You're next, Hogan," a voice summoned, interrupting my nervous chat with several other E-4s-in-waiting.

I swallowed a wad of spit, took a deep breath, and grabbed the doorknob. My previous week of preparation didn't prevent a swarm of butterflies from migrating in my gut.

In-country for five months, I wanted more money. Considered I deserved more. The additional 'Nam "combat pay" the army provided me helped, but hell, the army didn't pay me enough. Couldn't.

The army worked to replenish its ranks and everyone could advance, except the fuck-ups. And in a combat zone, advancement could come quicker, I'd learned. Advancement also meant higher pay. Many lifers, like John, extended their tours for the additional combat pay and the chance to rise in rank faster.

Bottom line, money and blood lubricated the war.

* * *

"You have an opportunity to interview for a promotion," Elliot announced to the three of us eligible E-4s in the office. "It's easier to get promoted here than Stateside." When John had left for "the World," Elliot assumed the position as our office enlisted man-in-charge. "Everyone gets scored and ranked according to performance, and competes with his peers. I'll give you several pointers."

Promotions flowed forth from the Pentagon, I knew, but for all I cared, the authorizations came from over the rainbow.

We gathered around Elliot. All of us wanted a leg up and Raines didn't mind. Besides, we weren't being diverted from anything critical at the moment.

Elliot started. "Interviewees ranked at the top receive promotions first, and so on down the list until the allocations are exhausted." After a short pause, he continued, "Don't pick your nose. Don't chew gum. Don't take a lit cigarette or carry any other item into the room. Present yourself dressed properly. Enter the room when, and only when, called. Move smartly to the chair provided. Salute and then—and only then—sit down."

Nothing new. The army loved starched, polished, and painted. That … and numbers.

He went on. "Sit straight, don't slouch. Look the interviewers in the eye and answer them directly. Avoid hand gestures. Don't fidget or bob your legs or head. Avoid slang. Don't cuss."

"Got it," I said. "At attention in the seated position, the living shit squeezed out of everything spontaneous. Smothered under drab-colored paint or made more complicated—one each, roll, paper, single-ply, toilet type."

Elliot looked at me, raised his eyebrows, and tilted his head forward. "They'll ask you, 'What's the proper location of your name on your belt?'"

"Inside the belt close to the buckle," I said.

"No, not good enough," he said. "On the inside of your belt, starting two inches from the end and marked in bold black letters on white background."

Trivial. "Why so damned important?"

"Just is," he said, "so memorize that response."

What's the big deal, anyway? NVA or VC intent on stealing my belt?

Elliot capped off our pep talk. "That's all. Break a leg."

Already fleeced of a field jacket, the army concerned I'd surrender my belt for redistribution in the field? A huge black market in belts I haven't heard about? Belts are belts, not nuclear weapons or bags of cash. Why not more emphasis on field jackets?

* * *

The door closed behind me, I approached my five inquisitors seated behind a long table, saluted, and planted my ass in the single empty chair that faced them.

Their questions began. Matter-of-fact and nonthreatening.

I began answering as best I could. *Give me a pay raise as soon as possible, please.* My hands gestured to emphasize and punctuate my statements, moved by an unseen puppeteer, a forgotten ancestral Italian part of me, perhaps. *Stop with the hands, dumb-ass.* But despite my best efforts otherwise, my hands had a mind of their own. My usual façade of control cracked, my frustration with the army and 'Nam oozed forth. My thoughts raced. *Aw, fuck it. I'm not a little sausage. Recognize me, a unique individual with a warm, beating heart.*

"Where is the proper location of your name on your belt?"

Ding. The magic question. Extra credit.

But before I started my response, thoughts of the army's obsession over that question jammed my head and my answer came out tentative and muddled. I'd botched the slam dunk.

"What's your opinion about the war?" one of them asked.

My opinion? That wasn't expected.

My ideas had begun to form before I shipped to 'Nam, built from newscasts, complicated by Basic, polished during my interaction with other GIs and locals in-country—the Vietnamese wanted peace, wanted to plant and harvest rice, to fish, gaze at the moon, write poetry, and make love. After all, though they were a different culture, they had similar aspirations as we Americans. I'd encountered intel reports that included excerpts from letters and diaries of VC poems and philosophy. Strange to think that Charlie thought about those things under the circumstances, but I wanted a future and sought ways to escape the war, and I knew Charlie wasn't that different from me … not really.

"Well," I took a breath and judged the interview panel mature enough to handle my opinion. "The South Vietnamese don't care who wins the war. They simply want the war to end."

The panel members looked at one another and nodded. With no further questions, they excused me.

What the hell had I done?

A RIGHT TO GROW IT

"The promotion results are posted," Elliot announced, a week after my interview.

On my first chance, I hurried to examine the results. My high hopes faded as my index finger moved down the names, one by one. Mine was in the lower half. "Fuck me," I mumbled. *Way to go, Bonehead, that's what you get for expressing yourself.*

Back in the office, Elliot asked me, "Check the board? How'd you do?"

"Didn't make the cut."

"Too bad. There'll be more promotions coming."

"Not soon enough," I said, pissed about my performance.

A shit-eating grin spread across Elliot's face. "I've chosen you for the inspection."

Damn it. He's rubbing it in. Sometimes I can't catch a break.

The shit-news about my lack of promotion didn't endear the army, the idea of an inspection, or Elliot's words, to me.

"A handful of enlisted men at Headquarters will stand for inspection," he added. His words confirmed the rumor floating around about an upcoming inspection by the Two Corps big cheese.

An inspection in a war zone is absurd. The general needs stooges to exercise his man-muscle? "Thanks for nothing, Elliot."

Kevin snickered. He'd arrived three months after me. Short and quick with words, he was the loudest mouth in the office, in my estimation. As he'd put it, he played "scrappy 'underdog' football in high school."

I'd always detested big-mouth know-it-alls. "Knock it off, dude," I told Kevin. Me, the sacrificial lamb, I'd need to shine my boots, shave every unauthorized hair, and put on fresh-starched fatigues.

The others kept quiet, avoiding drawing last-second attention to themselves, I figured.

* * *

The two-day advance notice of my inspection rendezvous with General What's-His-Face provided me time to prepare and rehearse, as if that would make any difference.

I leaned in, closer to the mirror. *I have a right to grow it.* Short whiskers protruded along a line above my upper lip—my mustache started two days before Elliot had delivered my summons.

Fed up with the army's haircut and shaving obsession, I wanted body hair, and as much as allowed, anywhere, preferably in plain sight. My lip-growth signaled my nonverbal "one-finger salute," directed at anyone whose ass chapped over facial hair.

I replayed my discussion about a week earlier with Top, our detachment's top-ranking sergeant. I'd approached him first thing after I'd heard the army allowed GIs to sport upper-lip hair.

"Top, I want to grow a mustache," I said, matter-of-fact and without hesitation.

"It can't extend past the corner of your mouth on either side," he said, also matter-of-fact and without hesitation.

"Why can't we grow beards, Top?" I said. "The navy guys can."

"Because you need a tight fit for a gas mask. Navy personnel aren't likely to need gas masks."

"I haven't seen a gas mask since Basic, Top," I'd said.

"Doesn't matter."

Well, ain't this a crap-fest.

I'd walked away with a small victory, far short of the one I'd hoped for.

I put on a clean set of jungle fatigues—light-starch only, please—and fresh-polished jungle boots, issued after I'd arrived in-country. Glad I didn't need to wear heavy-starched fatigues; I disliked the idea of chafing from cardboard shirts and pants. Everything had a trade-off: the light starch didn't hold creases long in our tropical sauna—maybe a day, though I'd stretch that to two days, sometimes three. I preferred jungle boots, lightweight, quick to dry, less black leather to polish, definite advantages over my Stateside clodhoppers.

ID on straight? I wiped my badge with my issue-green handkerchief. *E-4 rank insignia pins in the right places?* I adjusted the left one. *Gig line straight?* Gut sucked in, I tugged at my fatigue blouse until my shirt, belt buckle, and trouser fly created one continuous vertical line. *My shit's together.*

* * *

Fifteen minutes to eleven, Elliot told me, "Report for inspection in front of the Hotel."

Its all your fault I'm in that clusterfuck. I walked down the hallway at the pace of a dirge.

Out in the full sun, the glare assaulted my eyes though I wore my fatigue cap, which the army referred to as "cover." I eased into the middle of the milling herd of GIs.

A captain approached, prepared to eliminate our disorder and subdue untidy individuality.

"Form up in a single row," he bellowed. When we'd accomplished that, he ordered, "Dress right, DRESS!"

We adjusted ourselves to the man on our left, creating a straight line off that guy's right side.

"Atten ... hut," the captain barked.

Twenty young men snapped to, a token representation of all those within Two Corps Headquarters Compound. A slight breeze cooled me from behind and carried the scent of saltwater and seaweed.

I grew tense with anticipation that the general would interpret my hairy upper-lip as the badge of anger and dissatisfaction with the army that I intended it to represent, or would discover several rogue whiskers I'd not cut in my effort to push the boundaries. I harbored no illusion that my mustache would require care and coaxing to achieve a dignified status of manhood, however. *I could've shaved it off, but be damned ... I have a right to grow it.*

Everybody ready, General What's-His-Face appeared from the Hotel front entrance.

The captain looked nervous, no doubt concerned he'd get reamed, and saluted the general. "Ready for inspection, sir."

"Very well," the general replied, and started, paying special attention to detail.

Blennnd. Maybe my silent incantation could render me invisible to the general at the critical moment. But I ran through my checklist, anyway. *Don't move a muscle. Don't look at him or move your eyes. Don't make a sound.*

I could see him in my peripheral vision. Deadly serious, he performed his duty in a thorough, exact manner. Head-to-toe he checked each soldier, and when satisfied with one specimen, moved on to the next, sizing us up, his passion rivaled only by a bloodhound on a scent. He looked for anything out of place, the slightest imperfection that I imagined he'd consider a reflection on his character as a member of the US Army or his country, or that would determine the fate of the free world as we knew it.

Blennnd.

Military etiquette required silence while at attention. The one exception was to respond to your superior when, and only when, addressed. *Be extra nice, if he asks you something. And say, Sir, yes, sir … or Sir, no, sir.*

Braced, I felt light-headed, so reminded myself to follow the standard instructions for standing at attention. *Unlock your knees and blennnd.*

And then, there he was, Corp head honcho, right in front of me. Though I'd seen his approach, it felt like he'd materialized from thin air. He looked me over, up and down, his eyes on me the way I imagined mine would be on a young, soft-curved female I'd mentally undressed. *Is he getting off on this?*

He made the turn to walk on, but not quite fixated on the next man … turned back.

Oh shit, a slow-motion double take. Every muscle stiffened; my thoughts exploded. *Don't flinch. Don't giggle. Don't fart. I have a right to grow it.*

He leaned in close, dominating my field of vision, and fixated on my lip hairs, which had only emerged from my skin mere millimeters. I heard him breathing. On one side, then the other, he checked for one little hair out of bounds, as if my mustache intended to go rogue.

Did I miss something? I held my breath, not wanting to offer up any breakfast aromas. My body a coiled spring, I fought my urge to break rank, scream, and wet my pants, like a weak-kneed girl confronted with a squirming frog. *How long can I hold out?*

Without a word, he turned toward his next specimen.

I exhaled. *Get me out of here.* My heart throbbed in my neck and pounded in my ears.

Not more than twenty minutes after the affair had begun, the captain dismissed us before he followed the general into Headquarters.

As if released from the grip of a predator, I desired a secure place to hide. I craved anonymity and invisibility in case the urge struck the general to re-examine my upper lip. I feared he'd stalk me, or worse, have one of his minions order me to report to his office.

* * *

Returned to my worktable, I'd settled onto my stool.

Kevin looked my way, raised one eyebrow, "Hey, dude, you got mail. From your mom, looks like."

"I can figure that out for myself," I said.

I welcomed the delay in reading more classified reports and the distraction from the immediacy of my inspection.

Hi, Sweetie,

Mom's usual start didn't offend me. I needed reminders from home I'd not been forgotten. Her letter soothed me, like a bandage on an owie. I read her mini weather report and date in the upper right-hand corner.

Tuesday, Rainy, 58 degrees

That tidbit of information filled in a blank or two—cold, fat raindrops falling on grass and trees in our yard, and with a patter on the roof—and reminded me of my longing for home.

... I went to the funeral home to see Melba last week. She died of stomach cancer. You probably don't remember her. She married Henry, one of my third cousins. They lived in Greenfield. ...

Love, XOXO

Gossip and obituaries, Mom's way to reach out and touch me— the only way she knew how.

No way to escape reminders, my Corps HQ sanitized version of 'Nam-death, turned abstract by numbers, never shielded me from the reality that I might end up a statistic, too. When would my next brief random moment of blissful distraction usher me away and a shit-kick reminder jerk me back? But I looked to escape my 'Nam reality for fear I'd lose my shit and wind up nothing more than a warm puddle of piss in a corner.

I hung on in anticipation and with the hope of receiving my next bit of mail. Hoped more some days than others. My desire floated on an internal tide, subject to my preoccupation with immediate pursuits driven by hormones and desire to survive. Some days I got mail, most days I didn't.

As the hours passed, the realization grew stronger that I'd survived that inspection gauntlet, facial hair intact.

One small step for a general, one giant leap for Connard.

YEA, THOUGH I WALK …

"Now what?" I mumbled.

No way I could predict the timing of a summons from Gaston. From time to time he wanted me to show him a report or have me file one away. I considered him an unfortunate pain in my ass. Not a flaming asshole, the major, but still, I preferred to avoid him. I preferred to avoid any officers—all officers—including most of the lifer noncoms.

As I approached, I noticed Gaston intent at his desk. "Hogan here, sir."

He looked up. "Hogan, I need to brief the CO."

Mr. Big-wig?

He pointed to a whiteboard with grid marks that created a field of little squares, each containing a diagonal line. "I'll use this."

Major's busy little board.

Gaston rested the chart on his desk, held it there with one hand, and made broad strokes with the other. "I want you to identify each province across the top. On the side, put 'Confirmed VC KIA' here, 'Captured VC' here, and 'Fortifications Destroyed' here. Put last month's figures above the diagonal lines in each square and this month's figures below." He looked at me, "Got it?"

"Yes, sir."

The biggest project he'd requested of me to date involved VC dead counts. No surprise. About every other piece of information the army wanted involved the number of VC or NVA we'd killed.

With the major's tote board under one arm, I beat it out of his office and began to recall images of evening newscasts about 'Nam since my junior high school years. I remembered newscasts that focused on the number of Americans killed and wounded during that past week or month, or the tally since we'd entangled ourselves in that mess. Seduced to watch, TV had brought 'Nam into my living room every evening, up close and uncomfortable.

Back at my table, I recalled TV scenes of GIs jumping into waist-high grass with weapons (locked-and-loaded, no doubt) and wounded soldiers replacing them on the waiting choppers. Who among them had died? I recalled awesome scenes of B-52's dropping bombs and the succession of explosion-shockwaves in the jungle far below. I remembered the footage of an ARVN—Army of the Republic of Vietnam—officer in a Saigon street, who'd approached a suspected VC commander. It was impossible to shake the image of the captive's face, hands bound behind him, when the ARVN shot him point-blank in the head, administering a brutal summary execution. I recalled Dad's mention of the savage bloody battles on faraway beachheads in the Pacific, like Peleliu.

"Hogan, taking a nap?" Elliot asked.

"No, no." I focused myself on the tally board, beginning to label the categories and form the digits that represented our best estimates about Charlie's demise.

Each triangle provided every number a home, protected from intrusion from all the other numbers on Gaston's board. *The higher-ups are desperate for VC body counts.* Numbers came to be the measure of our progress in the war, distilled bottom-line numerals, representing VC and NVA bodies and the numbers of dead on their side versus ours. "Kill ratio," the army called it. *Yeah, Gaston wants numbers.*

The army salivated over numbers. Had there been any other way to gauge our progress in 'Nam?

* * *

Mid-afternoon, I finished Gaston's board and examined my handiwork. *Good to go.*

Easel tucked under one arm, I headed to the major's desk.

"Here it is, sir," I said to Gaston as I offered it up.

After a glance, he said, "No, this isn't right, Hogan. Your math is all wrong. I expected you to do this correctly." Gaston pointed out one mistake.

Okay, one little mistake. What's your problem, dude? Promotion on the line?

He found a second mistake, then a third. "You need to stop picking your nose, Hogan, and learn how to add."

No need to be a total ass, Gas Bag. Regardless of the condemnation of my work, there was no choice for me but to bite my lip, stand there, and suck it up.

He erased the offending numerals, replacing them with new, fresh ones done with a draftsman's precision. Gaston's review of the board completed, he told me, "You're dismissed. I'll keep the board."

Yeah, keep close rein of your precious board until the briefing, lest I fuck it up again.

Back at my desk, I reviewed a fresh batch of intel reports for my section, stewed over Gaston's reprimand, and waited for my next summons.

Late afternoon and about finished with my day's grease pencil updates on my map board, Elliot entered the office with a guy I'd never seen. Tall and slender, the guy had a prominent Adam's apple, while red hair highlighted his pale complexion.

Another FNG starting his tour as I had. How many days ago? Weeks? Didn't matter much, regardless, and I didn't want to be reminded.

"Listen up, ladies," Elliot said. "Meet Ray. Help him get settled in."

I needed a break anyway, so I approached, offered my hand, and said, "Welcome, Ray. Where are you from?"

"Montana, Big Sky Country," Ray said in a soft-spoken voice. He pushed his dark-rimmed glasses up his nose with his left hand, which betrayed a slight tremor as he gave me a solid handshake with his right.

Paired with the office short-timer he'd replace, Ray started his orientation, much like I had with Rudy.

For the rest of our work day, I watched our office newbie, Ray, off and on. I determined him the nervous type, but mellow and friendly—not an idiot, nor a flaming asshole or Kevin-type know-it-all.

* * *

My reprieve of several days from Gaston and his numbers ended with a call to report.

In front of Gaston's desk, I said to him, "You requested me, sir?"

"We need updated figures on the chart," he said. "Bring me your latest numbers."

"Yes, sir." *No fucking way to please you?*

We reworked the board, inserting fresh numerals with a new round of scrutiny. Gaston examined each triangle, all of which took on different values as other numbers shifted.

So much fuss over so few numbers. Heart attack or stroke on the way, major?

One triangle at a time, the major subdued the out-of-date numerals. Normal color returned to his face and I relaxed a little, too. "I need an assistant in the briefing tomorrow. I want you to come with me."

What? No wiggle room. Can't refuse a major. Another encounter with General What's-His-Face? My mustache, remembered from last week, trigger a fresh round of scrutiny? Opportunity to redeem myself for math failures with the major? I certainly didn't want the major to grow a bigger case of the ass at me.

"Well ... did you hear me?" he said.

"Yes, sir."

Gaston continued, "You'll hold a wooden pointer to the correct triangles on the chart, and I'll explain the numbers and attend to the general's questions. Understood?"

"Yes, sir." *Point man?* Though not the same as a point man leading a single-file column through the jungle, I'd still be under potential scrutiny from the general. I imagined myself exposed and caught off guard by something I could not foresee, much like my childhood experiences witnessing drunk-Dad's wrath. Everybody in 'Nam knew the point man usually got cut off from his group before being blown away in an ambush.

* * *

The next morning I made sure to put on fresh fatigues and clean underwear.

When the hour approached, I reported to Gaston as ordered. He looked pale. *Put on clean undies, too, Major?*

Easel, tally board, and pointer in tow, we waited on a bench in the hallway outside the Corps Commander's office.

The CO's aide, a corporal, summoned us on the minute in a perfunctory voice. "Come in, the general will see you now."

I tensed. Once again I'd be face-to-face, within whispering distance, of "the man," the nearest thing to God in Two Corps—a lieutenant general, three stars ... commanding. No doubt the slightest dissatisfaction from that guy, if I offended him, would grow while rolling downhill, and a shit-load of woe would fall onto me. That guy could banish me to Firebase Shit-Out-of-Luck in the Central Highlands then and there, if I pissed him off bad enough.

A wave of cool air blasted my face and bare arms as I followed Gaston through the door. *Air-conditioned? Luxury in the lap of swelter!*

Never having been in a general's office before, I wanted to feel cool and calm on the inside, but imagined myself the Cowardly Lion headed down the corridor to meet the Wizard of Oz. I cast the major, within arm's reach ahead of me, as Dorothy.

A wooden desk and office chair occupied one wall of the reception room, where I presumed the aide spent the majority of his time. He appeared to be in his mid-twenties and was dressed in crisp khakis, in contrast to my fatigues. His boots were spit-polished to a mirror's reflection. He even had his own swivel chair and desk!

Cush job for an enlisted guy. How'd he manage this? Become a lifer? Kiss whose ass? His daddy buy a congressman?

Gaston and I crossed over a floor rug in the reception room.

Yea, though I walk through the valley of the shadow of death ... .

In the general's office—the inner sanctum—I noticed a wooden desk and office chair, both larger than his aide's, and realized nothing appeared out of place.

Nice pad. Great to get to work in air conditioning. Wouldn't need to roll up my long sleeves, but wait ... anal-fixated officer alert. I'd rather slave in a place without upper-rank officers and avoid ulcers, thank you. I couldn't imagine working around higher-level officers without constant worry about screwing up somehow in their eyes. They had control over me; I didn't. And the higher their rank the more control they could wield.

Gaston and I set up his chart.

Armed with my wooden stick, I positioned myself near the board. Then ran through my checklist. *Breathe. Keep your knees bent. Booger in sight?* None that I could feel. *About to odorize the room?* Nothing on the way as far as I could tell. *Everything's clinched, up tight and out of sight.*

From their chairs, the general and several lower-ranking officers— the general's aides, I guessed—focused their attention. But regardless of their positions, ranks, or purpose, I also needed to remain focused, lest I end up cut down in an ambush. I stood, muscles quivering, stick in hand, groomed to point to those numerals on the chart and guide their eyes to the correct numerals. My orders were to help focus the officers on those little, well-drawn, unpretentious digits that meant so much to Gaston.

The major began. "Blah, blah, blah … as you see in the first square … blah, blah … ."

Tap! I placed the pointer in the correct square and applied some pressure to hold it in place, lest it move.

Avoiding eye contact with my higher-ups, I focused on the board and Gaston's words.

I shifted the pointer to a different triangle in concert with Gaston. *Tap!*

Gaston continued, "Blah, blah, blah … ." From the corner of my eye, followed by glances each time I'd relocated the pointer, I noticed our audience remained attentive, and I detected nothing untoward starting to brew.

Tap, tap! As I began to relax more into my duty, I emphasized a particular number in rhythm with the major's words. Did he like my flare?

The digits on the chart still added together, remaining perfect and unchanged since the major last examined them in my presence.

I remained conscious, though my brain pickled in a broth of adrenaline. I had a growing sense that I was doing a good job, while I tappity-tapped the pointer through the major's rendition of blahtity-blah.

After we'd reviewed all the numbers on the board, Gaston asked the general, "Any questions, sir?"

Gaston answered a few minor questions—I thought they were, anyway—with the mindfulness of a mother cat moving a newborn in her jaws. I heard no outright objections, and observed nodding approvals accompanied by subtle smiles. Most importantly, the general appeared content.

"That will be all," he said.

The major and I, excused from the old man's office with easel, chart, and pointer, headed down the hallway. Back in the land of mere mortals, I took a deep breath, glad I'd gotten though it mistake-free, and thankful I hadn't embarrassed myself with a loud belch or fart.

* * *

Back at my desk and somewhat settled after the briefing, I crossed my fingers in hopes of avoiding a third close encounter of the "general" kind.

"Hey, guys, I'm going to Da Nang," Kevin crowed, like an overgrown kid headed to Disneyland.

Da Nang was north, located in marine territory bordering the DMZ. And we all knew that the DMZ separated the South from the North, although for all practical purposes that wasn't worth the paper on which it had been drawn.

Remember the frequent attacks on the air base there, you fool?
"Going on vacation, Kevin?"

"Jealous?" he snapped.

"No, you go ahead. Don't worry about me." Not keen on Kevin's bravado, I'd learned to tolerate him well enough in the office to avoid outright conflict, which was unacceptable, though we sniped now and then.

"I can buy Montagnard bracelets and Ho Chi Minh sandals," he announced for everyone in the office to hear.

"Bracelets are cool," Steve said. "The Montagnard give them as a gesture of friendship."

"How much will that run?" I asked.

"Oh," Kevin paused, "give me a few bucks for each. I'll return anything left over."

"I'm in," Steve said and forked over a few MPCs. "Here's some moolah. General plunder and pillage isn't an option, and I probably won't get a chance to lift any souvenirs off a VC."

"Risky, like a drug deal," Paul said to Kevin. "But it all depends on who you buy them from."

"Yeah," I chimed in. "From Montagnard craftsmen, I hope, and not anyone who carries an AK to hunt GIs. We wouldn't want you to get captured by Charlie."

All of us had read reports of Montagnards who worked against the VC and NVA as a result of long-stewed resentments.

Kevin shot me a sideways look. "No problem. A buddy of mine up there has a good connection."

* * *

Several days had passed.

Elliot interrupted my study of a report with, "Hey, guys, the Avon lady's here with your beauty products."

Kevin laid the goods on his desk, consulted his notes, then distributed everything.

I put on my new bracelet—bent eighth-inch polished brass wire, and examined the chevron hash marks cut into it. "Not girly," I said.

Kevin laid a pair of black rubber sandals on my desk. "Here's yours."

Tire treads on the bottoms added to their sturdy appearance. "So, that's a pair of Ho Chi Minh sandals," I said. The unmistakable thick smell of rubber already filled the air.

"The latest fashion," Steve said. "Model them for us."

Squeaks of rubber on linoleum accompanied my walk around the room. With no arch support, my feet soon ached. "Damn, I thought army boots were bad."

"Perfect for wet, warm weather; they'll probably outlast you," Kevin said.

"Watch your language, there," I shot back.

"You know," Steve added, "Charlie shops for tires from downed planes in the jungle."

"Yeah, but tires are only a small part of our waste in 'Nam," I said to Steve. The bracelet on my arm and sandals set aside, I looked at Elliot and said, "Back in a minute. I've got to wash my hands. They stink of rubber."

"Too much for you?" Kevin quipped.

"Zip it, Kevin," I said.

At the washbasin mirror, I summed up the war. *Tire sandals symbolize Charlie's life, and polished black-leather boots symbolize mine.*

A PRIVATE WAR

I needed a sex fix, so I checked in with Steve as I prepared to leave the office. "Hey, interested in a trip downtown tonight?"

"Can't go until I'm done with babysitting, but I could meet you somewhere."

I knew the way. Caution laid aside, I said, "That's okay. I just need a quick trip." *Am I getting too cocky?*

After a clean-up and some chow, I headed out of the Compound on a beeline for the nearest brothel.

* * *

Satisfaction gained, I started back to the Compound at a fast clip.

Without warning, tiny hands grabbed me from behind and probed and pushed me, while loud yells of "GI, GI, GI," peppered me like machine gun bullets.

I pulled my arms loose and lurched forward enough to separate from them, then ran several steps. I noticed my Seiko watchband hanging loose, then discovered the button undone on the rear pocket flap of my fatigues, though my wallet remained.

I turned to assess the situation and stared down a height-challenged mini-mob.

"Get away from me," I yelled at the chest-high bandits. I threatened to chase them with repeated lunges until they hesitated and turned away. *Should've waited for Steve. Wouldn't have happened with a wingman alongside.*

* * *

First thing the next morning, sweating bullets, I reported for sick call.

"Hmm." The doc stayed calm, matter-of-fact, and objective in his exam and analysis of that particular part of me before delivering his professional opinion. "I'm not sure what that is. I'll refer you to a specialist in Cam Ranh Bay."

Oh, God. "You're not sure, sir?"

"No. We'll cut orders for you. It'll take a few minutes. Get dressed and take a seat in the waiting room."

Bad news for sure, I stared at my open sore before I pulled up my drawers. *Doc's unsure? They'll cut orders in a few minutes? What have you gotten me into, Mister Dick?*

Rumors of the Black Syph had dampened my enthusiasm for rampant sex but hadn't stopped my regular recreational forays with Steve to Nha Trang brothels, driven by thoughts that I'd explode from the crotch every morning.

Tap, tap, tap! My feet pounded out a steady rhythm on the linoleum floor while I watched the clerk type.

Within the half-hour, I held my papers—the doc's orders to proceed to Cam Ranh straightaway. I double-timed to my office, not bothering to grab any personal items on the way. "I have orders to go to Cam Ranh," I informed Elliot. "Medical reasons." My medical orders trumped everything else, and there was no way I'd go into the details. "I need a ride to catch a plane."

* * *

"What the hell happened?" Steve asked as he drove me to the air base.

"Serious shit ... but I don't want to talk about it, man."

"Okay," Steve said, and let me ride in silence until I hopped out of the jeep. "Take care," he said. "See you when you get back," he added, his usual mischievous grin absent.

"Yeah. See you, buddy," I said. Hoped I see him again. Hoped I'd return to Nha Trang and not end up in a hospital where I'd succumb to some unknown, incurable disease.

* * *

A C-130 cargo plane taxied to a stop.

An enlisted guy in air force fatigues and earphones hung around his neck gestured. "This is you," he said. "Follow me."

"Sure thing."

He led me through warm propeller wash to an open side door near the rear of the plane and pointed. "Sit there."

Without a studied glance I sat down and strapped in. The heavy-sweet, nauseating smell of antiseptic filled my nose, though better than the choke of thick exhaust I'd hurried through before I climbed in.

I looked up. *Jesus shit!*

I'd taken the last unoccupied space on a converted medevac transport. Stretchers of wounded GIs, several high and suspended by webbing, filled the plane's cargo bay. Tubes connected wounded guys to blood and other fluid bags. Bandages and plaster casts, a patchwork of white mixed with army-green and flesh, stood out in the dim light, a flying hospital ward crammed with the torn and broken.

I spotted a head bandaged on one stretcher, then a face bandaged on another. Traction devices of wires and pulleys suspended limbs—an arm there, a leg nearby, then an arm and leg on the same stretcher.

Marionettes.

Those I saw looked awake, avoided eye contact. Instead, they looked into an unseen distance. *What part of hell have these guys gone through?* I'd never been face to face with the "thousand-yard stare" before, though I'd learned about it from WWII movies.

There I sat on a medevac, a case of VD, but there'd be no purple heart for me. *If they only knew.* I nearly laughed. Wanted to tell the guy closest to me, his leg bandaged and in traction, but I stifled my urge. Those guys deserved respect and reverence for the wounds they'd suffered. They weren't joking or laughing. They weren't chitchatting. I accepted that each one was withdrawn deep into personal space, escaping into a different reality or being transported back to "the World" by pain medication and their memories.

Will any of these guys return home in a body bag? Will I end up a leper?

Quiet, I looked at the carnage as the engines droned and carried us south and away from Nha Trang. More self-conscious, I stopped looking at them; instead, head down, I stared at my boots. *Wouldn't trade my situation for theirs. Would they trade theirs for mine?*

Maybe ... maybe not. They held one-way tickets home, back to the States. And it dawned on me that they were the lucky ones. They'd avoided a body bag ... up to that point.

* * *

Fifteen minutes later, we arrived in Cam Ranh Bay.

Next to the door and still in control of my limbs, I beat a hasty exit. With no time wasted, I requested directions and headed straight to the appropriate medical building.

"I have orders to see the medical specialist here," I told the E-4 receptionist.

"The doctor's not in," he said. Didn't bat an eyelash. "He'll return in the morning."

No!!!! "Tomorrow morning?"

"Come back at eight. You can stay there tonight." He pointed to a row of barracks nearby.

Son of a bitch.

A raised-slat walkway, created by a string of pallets laid end to end, pointed the way. I heard faint muffled voices, but saw no one, which suited me. I didn't want to talk to anyone about my situation other than the doc.

Except for a quick trip to the mess hall for dinner without undue discussion with anybody, I spent that night in an empty barrack, squirming on my chosen bunk in my fatigues. I checked myself, then re-checked. Had to. Each time confirmed my worst fear that my open wound hadn't shrunk and, if anything, had grown. I pictured my most recent sexual partner. "Damn you," I yelled. I wanted to trash that barrack but knew that would do me no good and I'd pay big-time for any damage, sure I'd get caught. *My fault, anyway. I'd picked her out and paid her.*

I damn near prayed aloud for sunrise.

* * *

Out the door early, straight to and from breakfast, no chit-chat with anybody, I beat it to the doc's office at eight on the dot.

In the exam room within a few minutes of my arrival, the doc asked, "What's the problem?"

Pants and drawers to my knees, I pointed. "What is it, sir?"

"Hmm." He conducted a close examination before delivering his diagnosis. "I think I recognize this," he said without recrimination.

"If I'm correct, it's treatable with antibiotics and should clear up in a couple of days."

Thank God!

I watched him write the script, though couldn't make out his scribble.

"Give this to the clerk and make sure to take all the pills until you run out," he said, then offered me the small piece of paper.

"Don't worry, Doc."

"You're good to return to Nha Trang," he pronounced.

I offered my hand. "Thank you, sir." I would've kissed him out of gratitude, but that would've been awkward.

I passed the script to the receptionist forthwith.

"Hang on a couple of minutes," he said.

"I'm not going anywhere," I said as I watched him disappear down a hallway.

A minute elapsed before he returned with a medication bottle. "Take the first pill here. There's a water fountain behind you."

"What's in here, anyway?"

"Penicillin."

One quick swallow, my man parts saved—I hoped—not a moment too soon. "Which way to Nha Trang?" I asked.

He pointed. "That path will lead you to the landing pad. A chopper should arrive within the hour."

* * *

I waited alone on a bench aside the flat, graveled spot plenty large for a chopper to land. Somewhat hidden by shoulder-high brush that surrounded the area, concern over my medical condition took precedence over Charlie.

Curable. Not Dad's kind of war. Don't lose these meds. I double-checked my pocket.

About twenty minutes had passed when a Huey approached and settled onto the pad. Rotor wash blasted me with dust, rocks, and grass debris. A helmeted crewman motioned me forward and signaled for me to keep low to avoid the turning blades.

"Nha Trang?" he yelled, his words all but drowned by the deafening sound.

One hand pressing my hat onto my head, I shouted, "Yeah," as I nodded and climbed aboard.

No questions asked, not even to see my orders, he helped me—a solitary passenger—buckle in for my airborne limo service.

Fompf! Fompf! Fompf!

The chopper blades strained to lift us. Each thrust from the engine pulled us upward. In the meantime, we fell several inches.

Fompf! Fompf! Fompf!

Up, down, up, down, up, down.

Riding a glorified jackhammer with doors and seats.

With doors opened on both sides, wind whipped through the passenger bay and added to the roar.

Except for the reason I'd ended up on my first chopper ride, I was thrilled. On the other hand, I knew choppers got shot down all too often. I scanned nearby trees. *Charlie down there?*

We headed northeast, crossed a ribbon of beach, then cruised well out and over the water before turning north and paralleling the coastline.

Offshore from Nha Trang and compared to the shiny blanket of water surrounding it, the darker mass of Hon Tre Island drew my attention first. Hilly, vegetated—a perfect hideout for Charlie. Inland, beyond the long, blond beach, the military defenses of Two Corps sprawled south of the Nha Trang. Easy to spot, even at distance, I recognized the French Hotel, the primary structure within Two Corps Headquarters Compound. I scanned the patchwork of buildings and connecting roads closer by. I studied the airfield, bordered by military facilities and cordoned by wire fencing. I examined rows of barracks and scattered parked vehicles and artillery emplacements. I knew that thousands of personnel in U.S. units, alongside allied forces from Australia, South Korea, and South Vietnam, were spread across the area.

The tranquil scene of Nha Trang, as seen from the safety of distance—the cream-and-gray-colored buildings, deep-green vegetation, blue water, and khaki-brown dirt—resolved into a picture of the squalor of human survival in a war zone as we descended.

The chopper skids settled onto the tarmac landing zone at the air base. An obvious decrease in noise level indicated the pilot had switched off the engine, though the rotors continued to turn.

"Keep your head low," the crewman warned.

I nodded and said, "Thanks," before I jumped out. One hand atop my hat, I scurried away. My clothes flapped about. Every nerve activated, my body talked to me, as if I'd grabbed a live electrical wire. *My kidneys still attached?*

Within minutes, my nerves quieted and my kidneys stopped complaining.

A SLICE OF PIE

"Shit," I grumbled in the shower, a few days after my return from Cam Ranh. A fresh scar, a reminder of my indiscretion, had replaced the scab that had covered my wound.

Unable to put that discovery out of my mind as I worked at my office desk, I made a mid-morning trip to the latrine for a bladder break, where I confirmed the rearrangement of terrain on my private parts. "Fuck!" But I realized that was far better than the alternative, so I reminded myself that I should be grateful for modern medicine.

Headed back from the latrine, I ran into Steve in the Hotel hallway on his return from a mail run.

His usual smile absent, he said, "I got bad news from our clerk at Detachment Headquarters. As of today, Nha Trang is off-limits and we're moving."

"What?" I adjusted my stride to match his slower pace.

"Bad news, guy. We're restricted from Nha Trang. Overheard it at Detachment Headquarters."

Hit by that blind-side tackle, I asked, "Our access to local pussy gone?"

At that point, we'd come to a full stop in the hallway.

"Yeah. Ain't that a bitch?"

"Nixon's fu—" I looked around to check if any officers had overheard me. I saw no one but lowered my voice anyway. "That's Nixon's fucking Vietnamization program for you. Not six months in-country, not halfway, I'm restricted to military facilities. No more football on the beach. Worse, no more women."

"Looks like it."

I checked the hallway again. "Well, Richard can kiss my ass." I looked at Steve. "Moving us where?"

"Out by the air base."

"Why? What's wrong with the Compound?"

"A unit round-up, I guess, to a place called 'the Pie Slice.'"

"Our CO gathering us together, like little weenies in a can. I don't like it, just don't like it."

"Don't feel pregnant. Crap happens."

I pictured the small house that served as our Detachment Headquarters, a short jog from us at the French Hotel and separated from the beach-front road by a low rock wall—not even concertina wire as a token barrier. "I've wondered how our little Detachment building escaped an attack."

"Laughable, ain't it." Steve snorted. "Luckily, not on Charlie's top-ten list."

"Hell, a graffiti artist armed with a spray can could overrun it."

* * *

The next morning, as ordered, my barrack mates and I cleared out our metal lockers and stuffed everything into our footlockers and duffle bags in preparation for our relocation to "somewhere out by the airbase."

That afternoon, our gear in tow, we boarded two waiting two-and-a-half-ton trucks.

During Basic, I'd volunteered to help haul company troops and deliver hot meals from the mess on our company's field exercises in the boonies. In hindsight, that was the best decision I'd made in the army, other than signing up to be an Intel Analyst. We drivers referred those vehicles as "cattle trucks," and considered the guys riding in the back part of a mindless herd. "Those fools should've volunteered to drive!" we'd joke, especially on the coldest winter mornings.

Forced to be one of the herd now, I bid goodbye to my cocooned barrack and surveyed the surroundings out the open back of the truck as we left Corps HQ Compound. We turned south on the paved road along the beach front. Then, we turned right past the airfield, headed west through a cluster of wooden Vietnamese shacks, and slowed at a guard post where a gate limited entry.

"Why is this called 'the Pie Slice'?" I asked Elliot.

"Shaped like a wedge of pizza pie," he said.

We wound our way between rows of barracks. Weeds sought refuge against posts and buildings, out of reach of inattentive boots. A chain-link fence and concertina wire, eighty yards to the west, marked the perimeter.

Rice paddies, mosquitoes, and Charlie beyond that fence.

Our "deuce-and-a-half" slowed to a halt.

All the barracks looking alike made it hard to tell them apart. Horizontal wood planks overlapped from the ground up to waist-high and formed the outer walls. From his seated position, Elliot pointed to several buildings midway in a long row. "E-4's dismount here and move into those. E-5's will go with me to separate quarters."

Destined for E-5 housing, Steve remained in place, watching me as I climbed out past the lowered tailgate and unloaded my belongings. "See you around, guy," he said.

"Yeah," I replied, hating that we'd no longer bunk together.

* * *

I followed Paul inside the closest barrack.

Standard-sized pieces of plywood formed rudimentary cubicles large enough for two bunks at floor level, while a wooden footlocker and metal standing locker occupied each.

"I guess any bunk's as good as another," I said to Paul.

Wire screen, from the concrete floor to the roof's eaves, would block insects and allow air circulation. More open than the one at Corps Headquarters, it provided more space in which to move.

"Yay, partitions," I said. "Haven't enjoyed the luxury of these before. More private than our quarters in the Compound."

Other guys from our office trickled in behind us, fanned out, and started to choose bunks.

In the middle of the barrack, Paul staked his claim. "I'll bunk here."

I'd rather face Paul than Kevin. No time to ruminate, I said, "This one looks good to me," and claimed the territory across from Paul's bunk in the same cubicle. I realized that all that open space might make us more vulnerable in the event of an attack. *Safest in the middle of the herd, away from the doors. If Charlie barges in one night, it's about the same distance to the front or the back.*

A mosquito net lay draped over the attached metal frame of my bunk. Tucked in under the mattress all around, I'd enjoy a generous one-man mosquito-free zone. I glanced at Paul and said, "No jalopy spewing bug spray in the Pie Slice, I guess."

Standard procedure, I tested my bunk. It sagged under me. "Figures. This is like a fucking hammock."

"No surprise. Mine, too," Paul replied.

In hunter-gatherer mode and competing with other guys, I searched about for additional wood, plywood type, to place under my mattress. In luck, I spied and snagged a perfect piece from the adjacent bunker outside.

I sorted my several changes of civvies and military-issue uniforms. Then, using all of my hangers, I wedged them into my standing locker. "I've lived out of one of these metal lockers at least half my waking life since junior high school," I said to Paul.

"Me, too," he said.

My neatly folded socks, handkerchiefs, and underwear went into the lift-out drawer of my footlocker, same as in Basic and AIT. Snacks and a supply of pictorial entertainment mags went into the bottom, like a personal junk drawer. With its lid closed, my footlocker would act as a coffee table. However, I understood that things in plain view could grow legs and disappear in short order.

My decor, created from a careful selection of photos, a mixed *Playboy* and *Penthouse* motif—mid-to-late '69 period—and a poster depicting population explosion, personalized my plywood partition wall. *Ooh, that photo is a perfect crotch shot. I need a shower.*

A separate building housed the communal showers and private porcelain commodes, the same as those in the Hotel compound.

Thank God for flush toilets. No shit-burning in the Pie Slice.

* * *

My life had become one trapped within the confines of chain-link fences topped with barbwire, concertine type, around the Pie Slice, which was adjacent to the airbase and connected to the Hotel compound by jeep or truck.

I settled into my bunk for my first review of the latest copy of *Playboy* and a reread of Pam's newest letter, which had arrived earlier that day, about when I'd expected. With a slow pass under my nose, I checked for a hint of perfume on Pam's letter. Nothing obvious, but for sure no lipstick kisses on the outside. Pam lived with her parents and with no clue whether her mother read her mail, I didn't dare write about my carnal fantasies. No way. Our letters remained intellectual and philosophic, devoid of the suggestion of hot, steamy sex. But beyond that, I avoided talking about my feelings in general.

Having opted to turn inward in the face of Dad's alcohol-rages, I had grown up with a deficiency of emotional vocabulary. So, Pam and I stayed on neutral ground, though with every thought I pictured us "in flagrante delicto." I hoped she fantasized about me the same way. Regardless, her letters provided me with a reassuring sense of well-being about the present and future. I'd write Pam in a couple of days, according to our agreement to trade off a letter every week. *Where'd I put that Playboy?*

Bam! Bam!

"Incoming?" I yelled.

"No. You don't know they're from an artillery battery of fifty-fives?" Kevin said.

Bam!

"Stay in your hole, smart-ass," I replied.

By the second or third round, most of us could distinguish outbound from inbound.

Bam!

Another round hurried toward an unseen target. Our interpretation of hell on earth rained onto Charlie out there and pounded the hell out of him. No doubt he'd try to evade, run, or hunker down in a hole or tunnel, sometimes succeeding, sometimes not.

"It won't last long. An outgoing barrage usually lasts six to twelve rounds." Paul sounded confident about his observation.

Bam! Bam! Louder than a car backfire, though less than a bass-drum beat upside my head.

In a warm, dry bed separated from mosquitoes by a net, I felt pretty certain I'd get a cooked breakfast in the morning. Grunts and Charlie? Not so lucky. Once again, my decision to enlist and become an Intelligence Analyst didn't seem so bad at that moment.

* * *

Alone the next morning (barrack mates still at breakfast, or wherever), I waited at my bunk for a ride to the Hotel.

The front screen door screeched.

Clack! Clap, clap, clap!

I recognized the sound of flip-flops across the concrete floor. Wondering who could be short-stepping in a hurry, I stood up and looked over my plywood partition to find out. Dressed in a loose-fitting dark-brown blouse and matching baggy pants, a young female carried a handled wooden box and straw broom. A badge, pinned at chest level, along with the conical hat she wore, swayed at a pace with her steps.

We most often referred to the Vietnamese as locals or indigenous personnel. I knew they could enter the Pie Slice, provided they carried proper ID. A quick inventory of the box revealed cleaning supplies, rags, and cans of shoe polish. In a heartbeat, I pegged her as a local and not hell-bent to blow me up.

She made eye contact with me, smiled, came to a stop a few feet away, and set down her supplies. "I clean clothes, iron, sweep floor, dust, shine shoe." Soft-spoken, she sounded a little out of breath. "Cheap," she added for emphasis. Then she flashed her left palm, fingers extended. "I come fih time ... week."

A thin gold ring caught my eye. She stood as tall as my Adam's apple, about average for an indigenous. Straight black hair hung past her shoulders.

Brown eyes. Nice teeth. Smooth complexion. Mid-twenties? Pretty.
"I'll think about it."

With a big smile, she said, "I come tomorrow," then picked up her things and headed to the door.

Clap, clap, clap!

God, I haven't heard that kind of cheeriness in a long while.

Her baggy pants betrayed her butt-sway as she walked away.

Nice tail. I shouldn't try to take advantage, though. I respected her business hustle.

* * *

When he arrived at his bunk, I said, "Hey, Paul, there's a young woman who will come in and clean for the guys who pay her."

"What will she do?"

I repeated the points of her sales pitch. "Sounds like a good deal to me," I said.

Paul's eyelid twitched.

I had no idea why she'd walked into our quarters. Could've been we lived on her "street corner," by some arrangement determined between her and other locals. I hadn't asked, didn't care.

I went on. "It ain't that much money. Your area swept clean, civvies and fatigues washed, and boots shined in a combat zone? A no-brainer."

Paul gave me a slight head nod. "I probably will."

When she appeared the next morning, I told her, "Yeah, you clean for me."

She grinned. "Call me Mama-san."

Maid service! I'm moving up in the world. A little more sunshine had brightened my day, and I hoped a mortar round wouldn't punch through the roof.

Turned out most of the guys in my barrack hired her, too.

* * *

Settled onto my office stool, I got a summons to report to Gaston.

Crap.

138

"Hogan, I need to go to Da Lat for a briefing. I want you with me to assist."

Da Lat? My travel pace about to pick up? I'd been reassigned to cover that area of Two Corps in the Central Highlands, a French-colonial hideaway from the heat of the coastal lowlands. *Dangerous?* A snap response was called for—like I had a choice—once again subjected to the un-privilege of lower rank. The major was going and if hell bent, he'd order me along anyway. "Yes, sir."

"We leave tomorrow," he said.

I informed Elliot and the lieutenant in my office. Got no arguments from them. They couldn't override Major G. anyway.

* * *

A nondescript, corporate-sized turbo-prop plane covered in a dull, dark color taxied near us, no military markings to be seen. *Civilian plane? No, couldn't be. Air America, probably.* My office mates and I speculated about CIA secret operations within 'Nam. We received regular reports from one active "black program," and we understood "the company" worked on the QT.

The majority of the seats, more than I counted with a glance, remained empty when Gaston and I climbed aboard. No attendant appeared to usher the major and me to seats or offer drinks and snacks. Gaston motioned for me to take a window seat. He took the aisle.

Next to a window by the right wing, I remained glued to the view below and scanned the terrain for hostiles as we headed away from Nha Trang.

***

Inland, we descended onto remote flat terrain.

Zzzzzzzzzz! Our plane's tires announced touchdown on a metal-grate landing strip.

After we'd rolled to a stop, the copilot emerged from the cockpit, opened the exit door, and looked at the major. "We have a brief stop," he said.

The two only other passengers departed.

Through the small window, I looked out at the reddish-brown mud along the runway and the green fields in cultivation beyond the concertina wire perimeter. With no trees nearby, I had a unobstructed view several miles to the west, where mountains broke the horizon. Our plane sitting stationary and in the open on the airstrip gave me the creeps.

One passenger boarded.

With a rev of the engines we taxied and lifted off, continuing westward.

* * *

Two days in at Da Lat, Gaston and I did our military thing. Our briefings seemed a piece of cake, something familiar to me after my previous encounter with Two Corps Big Cheese. Nothing near as bad as my involvement in briefing a Three-Star.

Now, thinking back on that trip as hard as I might, I don't recall details of the military provincial headquarters in Da Lat or any briefings. I've blanked that out for whatever reason, though I know Gaston and I encountered no VC hostilities.

* * *

Upon my return to the office, Steve greeted me with a huge grin. "Hey, guy, I got my orders to go home."

With a bear hug, I gave him several pats on the back. "Great, good news for you." *Not good for me.* I looked forward to his leaving, only because I'd be closer to home myself, but I didn't look forward to office life without his devilish grin and jokes. "When do you leave?"

"Fourteen and a wake-up."

"All right! Short-timing it." I thought about the good times we'd had together. Realized our good times had occurred on the beach and in Nha Trang bars and brothels, before our relocation to Pie Slice perimeter-ville.

"Say, tourist, tell me about your trip," he said.

"A disappointment."

"Sow any seeds?"

"No chance," I said. "Stayed in the compound the whole time. Saw the Central Highlands by plane, though."

"You couldn't guess what I saw today," Kevin cut in.

"No, Kevin," I blurted, "but I'll bite. What?"

"A Vietnamese woman squatted on the side of the road," Kevin said. "Right there on the side of the road. Can you believe that?"

"Kevin … what would you do? Doesn't a brown bear go in the woods?" I looked back at Steve. "At least I didn't get my ass shot off." *But what about next time?* I couldn't predict when I might cross that invisible line between life and death.

Soon after our detachment relocation to the Pie Slice, a buddy examined an article of clothing at his bunk in the Spartan accommodations of our barrack. (Posters and X-rated magazine centerfolds appeared on various plywood partitions later as we personalized our cubicles!)

WHO GOES THERE?

I frequently recalled the words of one of my instructors at Fort Holabird: *In 'Nam, you're at the front, no matter where you are.* Like a shiv in my gut at the time, I'd remained acutely aware of his words.

The first night of my guard duty was bad enough. But my second night was worse; I was a zombie with weighted eyelids. The two-hour shifts, separated by rest periods of four hours, had worn me down and provided me no incentive to do anything other than sleep.

My stint at zero-dark-thirty had turned into a long fucking pull. Yeah, shut-eye was a need grown more pressing since I'd reported yesterday to a warehouse in a village on the outskirts of Nha Trang. I'd get released back to my unit tomorrow, but for now, my first guard duty in 'Nam—my only other time had been in Basic—ranked as one of the lowliest duties I'd been assigned. I considered it ranked above shit-burning, but just barely.

I had no clue what might occur during the shifts at my post. But with six-and-a-half months in-country, I had plenty of ideas of what crap Charlie could do. And by damn, I didn't want to get caught with my dick in my hand. Maybe, if I remained alert and noticed only one minor detail at a critical moment, I might live rather than die. I didn't dare take my situation lightly. I knew full well that one measly second could make the difference. And the other guys on duty with me would lay down lead pronto—if they stayed awake or hadn't already been hit.

Even with that in mind, little did I know what would happen.

* * *

A six-foot wooden ladder led up to my assigned guard tower box, which was covered with a slanted tin roof.

A whiff of wood, mixed with a heavy earthy smell, reminded me of my carpentry work on unfinished framed houses with Dad. I stifled a momentary wave of homesickness. Couldn't afford to get distracted. If Charlie ever took a shot, an AK-47 round would shred that plywood and tear me open.

The cold, wet air worked its way through my field jacket, nipped at my nose and ears, and turned my breath into a visible cloud. A deformed metal folding chair drained body warmth from my ass. I looked out over the eight-foot chain-link fence topped with coils of concertina wire with razor edges and points that made me cringe.

The guy in charge hadn't told us what we guarded; that information considered to be none of our concern.

Ammo or cases of three-point-two-percent beer? Surplus field jackets? Keeping whom from what?

A warehouse wasn't worth getting my tail shot off. I felt like a prisoner compliant with my own detention. But there was little chance any guy on guard duty, leastwise me, could sneak off with only one way in and one way out: through the guard house. I'd heard of GIs doing worse than leaving their guard post in 'Nam, though.

* * *

When I'd reported for my weekend duty assignment, a Brylcreemed crew-cut lifer, positioned at a cheap folding card table outside the guard shack, examined his papers, then ticked off the names of two guys ahead of me. Then he told them, "Plant your heinies, one each, on a bunk inside. That's where you'll be sleeping." Without a glance at me, he barked, "Next."

In freshly starched fatigues, I'd stiffened as if at attention. "Specialist Hogan reporting, Sergeant."

"Kissing my ass won't help you any, Hogan." He placed a mark by my name and without a look pointed over his shoulder with the eraser end of his pencil. "Grab a bunk."

Well, don't bust a sweat, dude.

* * *

Hunched down onto my seat and hunkered into my field jacket like a tortoise, I made myself as small as I could and prayed Charlie hadn't infiltrated the village opposite the airbase from Nha Trang. Hundreds, if not thousands, of Americans stationed adjacent to us should give Charlie pause. But I knew Charlie to be a bunch of fanatical, sneaky bastards.

I scanned the village in front of me, engulfed in a faint neon glow of fog, yellowed by floodlights that reached out beyond the fence and advertised my presence. Hooches, covered with weathered wood siding and rusted tin roofs, were lined up in rows. I noticed all their doors were shut and the dusty streets, if you could call them that, were empty. I saw no sidewalks, trees, grass, or flowers. Everything was meager and basic. Even the dirt looked poor.

One tower along the warehouse perimeter beyond mine claimed the "dead end" of our "dog run." The guy posted there, an even bigger thumb than me in my estimation, faced straight ahead, silent and motionless. Hard to tell if he remained awake. I could've raised my voice to talk to him, but didn't want to draw more attention to myself. Nor did I want to squander a chance to respond to anything, no matter how unimportant it may seem at first, so I didn't take my eyes off my sector except for an occasional glance.

In the other direction and closer to the guardhouse, but around the corner and out of my direct line of sight, I expected that Don occupied his assigned tower.

"Call me Don," he'd told me with a twang when we first met. "I'm just a skinny farmer from Alabama."

He'd looked squirrelly to me, but I'd liked him right off, though his introduction seemed odd. And I knew that when we were released back to our units after our weekend guard duty stretch, Don and I would probably never cross paths again.

Even with the proximity of my fellow guards and my loaded M-14, which I had authorization to fire, I felt isolated and at Charlie's mercy. *Fucking Elliot put me here.*

More than ready to climb down, I'd hustle to the corner fifty feet away given my first chance. Then, I'd trudge another one-hundred-fifty feet to my chosen bunk in the guardhouse. I considered my temporary housing a dungeon, crammed with dingy mattresses that reeked of the stench of mold, as well as a gaggle of farting, snoring males—some not past adolescence and steeped in their own B.O. In my wrinkled fatigues—that tidy, starched look so cherished by the army long gone—I'd hope sleep would overtake me in a New York minute … if nothing unexpected happened.

I checked my watch. "Crap, hurry up," I mumbled.

I assessed my odds of getting blown away. I knew they were far higher than a sapper's, which equated to about that of an individual eating a bullet compared to the odds of an engineering college sophomore back home. Charlie could pop off a few AK rounds from anywhere nearby, a sniper could take a long-distance shot, or a mortar squad could bombard me from beyond the village. A sapper had plenty of time to crawl up against the fence and cut a hole. Hell, one could approach me dressed as an old woman.

Everything quiet. Have all the dogs been eaten by the locals?

Home, my family, and even the nerdy guys proud of their slide rules and pocket protectors full of pens and pencils in my engineering classes may as well have been on the back side of the moon.

I glanced at my watch again. "Good, time to go," I mumbled.

I didn't want to spend another frigging second in that open plywood coffin. I stood, reached around to check if my numbed butt remained attached, then shouldered my weapon before I backed down the ladder. *Perfect time for Charlie to take a shot.*

I got the hell out of there, hurrying with long strides to the corner, wanting to get to my fucking bunk in the guardhouse. *Let Charlie come on somebody else's watch.*

At the corner, I reminded myself to turn left, as if that made a rat's-ass difference. There was no other way to go.

Don, down from his assigned tower, stood motionless in the rut of the four-foot wide dog run and faced outward toward the village. I'd expected to see Don's rear end as he headed for the guard shack.

As I drew closer, I heard high-pitched yells before I noticed a boy standing six feet beyond the fence with something clutched in his right hand. *What the fuck?*

Several seconds passed before I realized that the kid was holding a rock, not a grenade. About twelve years old, dirty and bare-skinned except for his tattered dark shorts, he appeared no major threat, as he didn't hold an AK or wire cutters. *On a personal mooching mission gone wrong?*

Don and the kid glared at each other, both remaining still until I closed to within arm's reach of Don. Then, Don raised his M-14 and aimed at the boy. "You little shit," he hissed. Spit accompanied his words.

Whoa.

The scrawny runt spewed a string of jumbled words at Don as fast as bullets from a 50-cal machine gun.

Don tensed. "I ought to shoot him." His blood-red face and bulging neck veins told me everything I needed to know.

With no idea how itchy his trigger finger had gotten, I measured my words in a lowered voice. "Don … don't do it."

Don's attention remained fixed on the boy. "The little bastard hit me with a rock."

Well, that little shit. I caught myself and said, "You don't want to waste him, Don. You could end up busting rocks in Leavenworth, man."

With muscles tensed, and prepared to heave his rock, that kid didn't back off. He rattled off another burst of words.

"What's wrong with that kid?" I asked Don, though didn't expect an answer. I glanced at the kid. *You got a death wish?* To avoid drawing his ire, I said under my breath, "I'd reach through the fence and smack the living shit out of you if I could, you little idiot."

I understood Don's reaction, perfectly. Who needed a bunch of shit screamed at you by some half-pint? It scared me to think how little it might take for me to pull the trigger, but I wasn't going to say that to Don. Besides, I wondered if my brain might just take a quick vacation-nap as I stood on my feet, and I guessed Don was no better off. Pretty hard to keep a clear head with sleep about to steam-roll you.

"Bag it, Don. Ignore that little fucker."

Don, quiet now, didn't move.

What we had was a regular Mexican standoff, and I didn't know if he'd even heard me, so I repeated myself. "Hey, Don. Bag it, man. Ignore that little piss ant."

Don remained focused on the boy. Slowly lowered his weapon, but stood in place. Easy for me to see his clenched jaw.

The boy stared at Don, quiet but defiant.

"Come on, man. Drop it." I took a small step. "Let's go."

"You fucking little bastard," Don yelled. He turned toward the guard shack, though looked back at the boy.

"Keep moving, guy," I said and stayed close behind Don to encourage him along. I glanced back several times to see what that pint-sized punk might do until I lost sight of him.

Don paused at the guard house door. "Thanks, man," he said. "I was ready to shoot that punk."

I laid one hand on Don's shoulder and said, "That little shit ain't worth it, man."

Exhausted, but unable to fall asleep until my adrenaline rush subsided, I replayed the episode, which had lasted no more than a couple-dozen seconds. *If not for me, Don could've wasted that kid. How many indigenous personnel had we blown away in other similar crazy-shit situations? And what had that kid been put through to have gone that far?*

THE GOOD, THE BAD,
AND THE UGLY

I'd settled onto my bunk, when Paul approached his and said to me, "Hey, I just found out there's a movie theater here. I think I'll go check it out. You interested?"

I needed a change of pace. Steve had stirred things up in a good way and, though more studied and quiet, I'd gravitated to Paul to fill my buddy gap in the evenings. Bottom line, I spread myself around, though in a limited manner, to cultivate a short list of friends as back-ups and vary my experiences.

A movie couldn't hurt. I turned the page of my newest *Penthouse*. "Yeah, I'll go. Know what's playing?"

My adjustment to the Pie Slice—a continent compared to the postage-stamp HQ Compound—took time, but little by little the gaps in my knowledge got filled.

"No idea. Didn't bother to find out," Paul said.

* * *

Paul and I claimed middle seats on one of the wooden benches near the back. Ruts in the dirt between the bench rows testified to the number of absentminded feet shuffled as their owners sat engrossed in fantasy.

The flat, slanted metal roof, supported by wood beams, sheltered the area from rain and blocked our view of the stars overhead. The screen faced the perimeter. In the open, separated from the surrounding buildings, we sat within clear sight of the base perimeter fence and beyond.

Eighty guys, give or take, gathered on the benches.

Charlie watch our movies, too? Good thing or bad thing? Enjoy Cool Hand Luke *or* Planet of the Apes*?*

As the opening movie credits began to scroll, I wondered how Charlie would react to the same film I was watching. Images appeared:

A rider on horseback crosses a desert.

As strange to Charlie as 'Nam jungle to me?

Three bad-asses have a face-to-face shootout in an empty street.

Charlie would never have a face-to-face shootout, if he could avoid it.

Blondie rescues Tuco from the town's people. But Tuco turns the tables and makes Blondie walk through the desert, then leaves him for dead.

What would Charlie think of this story of thickening greed?

Someone must've yelled, but I didn't hear what. Guys seated on the fringes jumped from their seats. The sound of anxious boots pounded the ground, echoing under the metal roof.

"What happened?" I said, though not to anyone in particular.

"Clear out," someone near me yelled.

An attack? I didn't hear any mortar rounds.

Those seated in the middle of the crowd, slowed by those closer to the fringes, jostled to scurry away. Off guard and unsure what had started the exodus but caught in the current, I followed suit. *Sappers inside the perimeter?*

The crowd, like a hatch of two-legged cockroaches, scattered in every direction. At fifty yards' distance, the guys nearest me slowed to a walk, then stopped.

"I heard a loud explosion," one guy said.

I listened to the relative quiet, turning my head for clues. "What explosion? I didn't hear an explosion." Mortar rounds, a common gift from Charlie, usually came in bunches after midnight.

"Sounded like a grenade to me," another guy said.

"Yeah, me too," Paul said.

The rumor moved among us, a proverbial bucket of water passed along a fire brigade, until it achieved the quality of fact.

"Some officer got fragged," somebody said.

I'd heard rumors of disgruntled GIs serving up live grenades to higher-ups, though hadn't known of it happening in the Pie Slice since my unit's relocation there. Though I wondered who'd been the target and if they'd caught some fragments or bought the farm entirely, that story was preferable to any about Charlie being inside the wire. So, I put my questions to rest, figuring I would hear details later. Several minutes passed as disorganized collections of individuals milled about, like a herd of dumbfounded ruminants after a stampede. I concluded that signaled the end of *The Good, the Bad and the Ugly*—for that evening, anyway.

"Paul, I need a drink," I said.

"I'm going back to the barrack," he said.

My chance to avoid the onset of stark-raving boredom, I headed for our detachment bar. Some of our enterprising enlisted colleagues had opened and manned the joint—must have gotten our CO's blessing—after we'd relocated to the Pie Slice. I didn't know those guys. They and I didn't run in the same circles, nor did we work together. Free enterprise in action, I figured—at least they were earning themselves some extra pocket change.

* * *

Credence Clearwater Revival's words, "I see the bad moon arisin', I see trouble on the way," greeted me when I opened the door to our rec room, on my way past the pool table to our bar cubbyhole in the back.

I pulled up at the counter next to Wesley.

"I'm from Chicago," he'd told me when we met upon his arrival several months ago. After that, we'd come across each other only now and then, since we didn't work in the same office, or bunk in the same barrack.

An iced drink occupied the counter, situated about the same distance from each of us. The glass, covered with sweat, engaged my attention and I imagined its sweet taste. *Wesley's?* With one hand I grabbed the glass from above and slid it in his direction. "Is this yours?"

Wesley glowered. "Keep your fucking filthy hands off my glass."

Whoa. "What's wrong with you?"

"I saw you pick up the glass with your filthy hand," he said.

Credence continued, "Don't go 'round tonight, it's bound to take your life, there's a bad moon on the rise. ... " The others in the room had gone quiet.

Shocked by his intensity, I said, "I only moved it over."

"How dare you? I saw you put your filthy fucking hands on my drink."

I'd stepped into a pile of shit, and no matter what I did or said, I figured things would stink. And though angered by his words, I wanted to avoid a mix-up, so I kept my mouth shut. *How about I frag your ass? Or slap the shit out of you?*

Within arm's length of one another, his jaw clenched, his nostrils flared, and I wondered if he'd strike out. He looked wiry.

I'd probably not even win that battle.

Although my run-ins with several guys in the army to date remained vivid, I considered myself open-minded, and devoid of prejudice against people in general. Thought so, anyway. I ordered a drink and bit my tongue. Didn't want to end up busted for fighting.

Wesley grumbled and bitched the entire time I sat there.

I felt sorely tempted to tell him to shut the fuck up but knew where that would probably lead, so I gulped down my drink and left. Decided I'd steer clear of Wesley. I knew if I hung around him, I'd be tempted to smear his mustache across his face.

I heard nothing more about that fragging incident. Figured the incident had turned out to be a relative nothing-burger.

THUMP! THUMP!

Thump!

    Roused from sleep, I thought, *What was that?*

Thump!

A collective GI consciousness stirred to attention. Another moment passed before urgent cries of "Incoming" echoed from scattered locations by guys yanked from dreamlands of heated fornication with eager young females, or the bliss of nothingness.

Thump!

"Mortars," Ray yelled from the adjacent barrack.

Should I move?

Thump!

Are they a safe distance away? Should I stay on my bunk?

Thump!

"Greetings from Charlie," Kevin yelled from across our barrack.

"We never dealt with mortar rounds at the Hotel," I said.

Thump!

"No. The Compound is five-star," Kevin replied.

Move? No creaking bunk frames. No footsteps across the concrete floor. With the yin-yang of indecision, I held my breath. My heart pounded. "Head for the bunker?" I called out.

Thump!

"You might not get there," Paul replied. "Roll out and crawl under your bunk if they get close."

155

Thump!

Another round had crashed into something solid.

Still a safe distance away?

A shift in the mortar's aim could put one anywhere, even right on top of me.

Thump!

Time to move? "Which way are they going?" I called out.

Thump!

"They're not walking this way," Ray yelled back.

Stay.

Thump!

"Let's keep it like that," I yelled, and appreciated Ray's ability to determine the direction the rounds "walked." I couldn't distinguish the line but knew Charlie lobbed his shells, trying to hit a valuable target. Random for Charlie, personal for me.

Ray's voice sounded less urgent. "I think it's over."

"Those were too close for my taste," I said to Paul.

"A couple of hundred yards away," Paul said, his voice calm.

I imagined a mortar round punching through the roof above me. "Welcome to the Pie Slice. Two weeks to settle in and Charlie threw us a housewarming."

A few scattered comments and nervous joking floated around before everyone grew quiet again.

I didn't know if was it safe to drift off to sleep. Safe enough to dream of a receptive girl and wet sex. To dream of the smell of fresh-mowed grass or warm-blanket Saturday-morning cartoons. How many attacks would it take to impact me in long-lasting ways? Who knew?

Reminded that Charlie blended, prowled in the darkness, and pounced when I least expected, I half-slept the rest of the night.

* * *

The approach of dawn triggered usual workday routines.

Mid-morning, settled in at my table at Headquarters, Paul returned from his mail-call run. "Hey, guys, I heard Second Lieutenant Cullins got hit by a mortar fragment last night."

I hadn't met him. "Wounded?" I said.

"Yeah."

"How bad?"

"I think it's minor," Paul said.

No body bag. No DOD condolences to a family.

"Where was he?" Steve asked.

"In his room. We can take a look after work," Paul said.

* * *

Back in the Pie Slice, Steve, Paul, and I headed to Cullins' quarters in an officers' barrack. Sure enough, Paul had been right about how far the officers' barracks were from ours.

Cullins lay flat on his bunk and on top of his army blanket, feet propped on the metal frame at the foot of his bed, a large white bandage and brace on his left foot, and a polished, black-leather boot on his right.

I couldn't help but gawk.

"We came to check out the damage," Steve said.

"The round came in there," Cullins said. He pointed toward one corner of his room where daylight shone through a baseball-size hole in the corrugated metal roof, visible proof that Charlie could've reached out and touched me if he'd aimed his rounds in my direction.

"I'd taken cover under my bunk right before the mortar round came in," he said, "but a fragment hit my big toe."

I nearly laughed but thought better of it.

Cullins went on. "It's a small wound, not much blood loss. Hurt like hell, but they gave me pain pills for it."

157

"A few more inches and that thing would've missed your room," I said. Easy for me, or anyone else, to see that.

"Hey, if you're lucky, you'll get sent home. Not a bad way to get the hell away from here," Steve joked.

"Yeah," Paul chimed in.

"Our CO told me I'd get a Purple Heart but not a trip home." Cullins grinned, cheeks red. His rounded facial features suggested a layer of baby fat.

ROTC wonder, no doubt, had sent him to 'Nam on a beeline straight from school.

Gouges spread across furnishings and walls. I imagined a shotgun rampage by a drunken, trigger-happy maniac.

"A few of your things got hit, too," Steve said.

"Yeah, my turntable and a few clothes, nothing important," Cullins replied. "There wasn't much damage done and everything can be replaced."

* * *

Outside, Steve shook his head. "Sure glad that mortar round didn't get me."

"Let's check out the impact craters," Paul suggested.

I spotted a bright silver ray of lines surrounding a small hole in the asphalt pavement. "I see one," I said.

We walked over for a closer look.

I couldn't help but think it had a brutal appearance. "A crater on the moon," I said. "Made a small hole in the road, but would've torn any of us a new ass. Charlie's message is loud and clear: 'Go home, you're not wanted here.'"

Steve gestured to create an imaginary line. "They came across here."

I gauged the distance between two craters to be about forty feet. "Yep, in line with Cullins' room. He's a lucky bastard," I said.

After a moment's pause, and with a step, Steve said, "Let's go eat."

I followed. "Tell me again, Steve, how short are you?"

"Ten and a wake-up."

"I'm envious, you short-timer," I said. "Wish I was going, too."

"You'll make it, buddy." He rested one hand on my shoulder and gave me a light shake.

I already missed him.

MAIL RUN

"Hogan, it's your turn to pick up our mail," Elliot said.

Yay, my turn. Mail run got me out of Elliot's sight. Caught up on reading my reports, I'd been wondering how I'd fill my day. Didn't want to give Elliot any excuse to assign me shit work. "Got it. No need to tell me twice. I'm out of here." I grabbed my head cover, as well as the key to the padlock that secured our office jeep, and skipped out of the office. *Free. Letter from Pam?* Neither paperwork, nor a hangnail, nor a call of nature would deter me from the completion of my appointed round, if I had anything to say about it.

Light-footed, I moved down the hallway, then bounded down the stairs. I began humming as I left the Hotel, then mouthed a few words: "Why don't you come with me, little girl ... on a magic carpet ride? Well ... you don't know ... ."

A few puffy clouds hung in the sky. I pulled my cap down to shield my eyes from the intense sun and climbed into the seat under our jeep's open canopy.

I gave the guy a nod as I eased the jeep past the Corps HQ guard post, then turned right for the long fishhook journey to our Detachment Headquarters in the Pie Slice.

Cooled by the blowing air and soothed by the shade cast by trees along the road—a strobe effect of shadow and light on the windshield ... off, on, off ... on, off ... on—I felt at peace.

Any excuse to interrupt the death grip of office routine boredom, I welcomed chances to get away from my desk, get out of the office, leave the French Hotel, exit the Compound, travel out of Nha Trang, for sure leave 'Nam ... above all, return to "the World."

Seven months in, far too much time left for me to start my countdown, I'd grown to feel that I lived on a short leash and the army owned my ass. Though that grated on me and left me angry and resentful, cooperation with the army remained my best protection from Charlie, so I'd opted for the subtlety of quiet passive-aggression.

I hadn't relished every reason to leave the safety of the office. Not for an inspection in the Compound by General Big Wig. Hell, no! No inspection, nowhere, no-how was worth it. No one I knew wanted to get inspected ... ever. Getting away on sick call was okay, though the reasons for it weren't. Never crossed my mind to feign or induce illness. I'd heard some guys did that to avoid jumps into red-smoke "hot LZs" (landing zones under fire). Some had done that to avoid humping recon in the bush on LRRPs (Long-Range Reconnaissance Patrols, which we pronounced as "lurps"). I guessed that they'd weighed the odds and concluded that their efforts were worth the risk of getting busted and being sent anyway. A summons by Gaston remained a mixed bag. I never knew when, and rarely knew why, until I stood in front of him. But I enjoyed the mail run.

Pleased with the traffic, light that time of day on the two-lane road, I anticipated the stoplight between me and the Pie Slice as my only obstacle. The smooth, shiny-black asphalt begged for an open throttle, but I resisted. I wanted to avoid an accident or a speeding ticket from the military police.

A prop-driven commercial plane landed on my right as I drove alongside the airfield. Hon Tre Island dominated the horizon off to my left.

Peaceful. Pleasant. I almost forgot I lived in a combat zone.

The Pie Slice entrance guard nodded to me after he saw the ID badge pinned to my fatigue blouse, and signaled me with a sweep of one arm to proceed. I acknowledged him in turn and eased through the gate. Within another quarter of a mile, I brought the jeep to a stop, turned off the engine, then used the heavy chain and padlock to secure the steering wheel.

Under the warm sun, I strolled across the forty feet of parched, dusty asphalt and hard-packed dirt to Detachment Headquarters and opened the screen door.

"I'm here to pick up mail for the Hotel office contingent," I said.

"Okay," our detachment clerk acknowledged, head buried in paperwork. He rose from his desk and took several steps to a bank of mail slots on the wall. With an index finger, he found the slot where he'd sorted our mail earlier that morning. He handed me the neat bundle with a "Here you go," and started back to his desk.

I assured myself I'd gotten the right batch. "See you later."

From his chair, he responded with a flat "Yeah," head reburied in paperwork.

In no hurry, mail safe in hand, I walked out of Detachment Headquarters.

Great weather.

The assortment of envelopes tempted me to leaf through them for my name, a letter from Mom or Pam, or anybody, with news of life back home. But I could extend my break from office routine if I waited for that discovery there. The bundle placed on the jeep's front passenger seat, I savored the possibilities, unlocked and removed the chain that secured the steering wheel, and turned the ignition toggle. Both hands and both feet engaged, occupied by separate and distinct tasks, I prepared to shift into first gear.

Shhzzz!

"What the hell?" I mumbled. "That plane's flying low."

SHHZZZ!

Hot-dogging? About to crash?
SHHZZZZ!!!

Close! I peered out from under the jeep canopy. Couldn't see it, but I heard the unmistakable doppler shift in pitch as it roared past. *Must've gone right over me.*

Shhzzz!

BOOM!!!

Several seconds elapsed before a voice from within detachment headquarters building screamed, "INCOMING!"

The jeep would provide me no protection. *Take cover.* I cut the engine as my heart revved. *Chunks of metal, wood, or body parts rain from above? My last day? Blend into the dirt. Charlie at the perimeter? The jeep? The mail? My last day?* With fingers-turned-thumbs, I worked the limp, steel chain. I didn't want to pay for an army jeep stolen while in my possession. I held my breath, listening for anything more than the rapid thump of heartbeat in my ears. *Don't hear anything. Get out of the jeep, dumb-ass.*

Ten seconds, maybe twenty, elapsed in my time-warped universe before I threaded the chain, long enough to wish I could watch Saturday-morning cartoons as a kid again.

Padlock in place. *Click!*

The jeep secured, I hauled ass. *Another one on the way?*

To the nearest bunker in a dozen steps, as fast as I'd ever run. With a weave to avoid the sandbags guarding the entrance and a head duck, I lunged inside, football-receiving skills put to excellent use.

Alone and winded, with most of my unit's personnel oblivious at Corps HQ, I guessed our Detachment CO, Top, and clerk had taken cover under their desks. As the sole occupant, I had run of the bunker, so I claimed a position in the middle of the crude, man-made womb of mother earth. Big enough for forty GIs to huddle and stay warm—more than enough space for me to lounge.

More in-coming?

Cool air carried a strong, heavy odor of molded wood and dust, thick enough to taste. Wood planks in the central trench would prevent footsteps into a muddy quagmire during monsoons.

Another one on the way?

I visualized the thick sandbags and a layer of dirt covering the plywood roof above. My sense of safety deepened. Not a total reassurance, however; a relative one, and at that point I blended into that blessed bunker.

Idiot. Who would've stolen the jeep?

Ten to fifteen minutes passed without other explosions, gunfire, or urgent, desperate cries. "All clear," someone from inside Detachment Headquarters yelled, signaling the resumption of usual routines.

Out of my shelter, reborn, exposed, bombarded by bright light, cap down to shield my eyes, I headed back to the jeep.

The pile of office mail lay undisturbed on the passenger seat. I didn't dither, didn't hesitate one iota to escape from the scene.

Past the Pie Slice guard gate and off to the left, about one-hundred-fifty yards from where I'd parked the jeep, a black-soot cloud billowed several hundred feet into the air. Flames danced up the side of the slender, 50,000-gallon aviation fuel tank that towered over the cluster of nearby hooches.

I crept by the scene at an idle in low gear and took a mental photo. Caught a whiff of burnt fuel and saw no one in sight. Firefighters had yet to respond.

Damn big ... whatever it was.

It had been barely a week since Cullins got hit. Was Charlie upping the ante?

* * *

Back in the office, I handed our day's mail straight to Elliot. "Here you go," I said. "I need to sit down."

Before I got to my stool, Paul asked, "Hear the explosion?"

"Hear it?" I said. "The fucker, whatever it was, flew right over me after I came out of Detachment Headquarters. I hid in one of our bunkers after it exploded until the 'all clear.' The fucker made a direct hit on the aviation fuel tank."

"They've identified it as a Katyusha rocket," Paul said.

"Asshole Russians. In high school I learned they bombarded the Nazis during World War II with clusters of those. They'd nicknamed them after a Russian folk-song heroine, Katyusha, who missed her lover, gone off to fight."

Kevin cut in. "Our bunkers can stop mortar rounds, but not rockets. Maybe they can stop artillery rounds, although Charlie doesn't operate artillery, at least in this part of 'Nam."

"Yeah, tell me something new," I replied. "Regardless, he hauled that Katyusha here, didn't he?"

Empty-handed after Elliot passed out the last piece of the day's mail, I shuffled paperwork at my table and rehashed the event. Only Charlie knew his intent when he fired that thing ... but if it had fallen short? I'd presented as one juicy target there in the jeep. *Damn you, Charlie!*

THE WESTERN FRONT

Two distant explosions interrupted my after-dinner contemplation on my bunk of that fucking Katyusha rocket earlier in the day.

"Hey, guys, come check this out," Kevin's irritating voice yelled from outside our barrack.

I looked across our cubicle at Paul, who was on his bunk holding a magazine. "I wonder what that's about."

Headed toward the door, I heard a clamor on the metal roof. Outside our barrack door, I said, "Where the hell are you, Kevin?"

"Up here," he replied. His head popped into view past the edge of the roof.

"What's up?" I said.

Paul stopped beside me.

Kevin pointed west. "Two jets taking turns."

The eastern flank of the mountains lay in the evening's heavy shadow. A horizontal gray cloud of smoke, pushed by a wind, spread out, while another mushroomed upward.

"I've seen pictures of caves up there," Paul said to me. "I'll show them to you tomorrow if you want."

Opportunity to watch us give Charlie shit. "I'm going up," I said to Paul. "I've never seen a plane drop bombs, except on TV and in the movies."

One jet made another pass. With an orange flash, a new cloud appeared.

I counted out the time. *One second, two seconds, three—*

Boom! A low rumble echoed off the distant mountainside.

"Take that, Charlie," I yelled.

Ray climbed up and sat next to me.

Each plane maneuvered in a wide circle as the other made a run. We watched for ten minutes before both planes joined up and headed toward the air base together, the runway a mere few hundred yards from where we perched.

The smoke merged into one long, thin cloud.

I hadn't kept track. "How many bombs did they drop?"

Ray spoke up. "I counted eight."

Kevin pointed. "Look, there's another plane headed that way."

Hard to see, another plane lumbered toward the mountain.

A burst of crimson ribbon emerged from it over the spot where the bombs had fallen. As if blown by a gentle breeze, the ribbon twisted and snaked to the ground in silence, crisscrossing the bombed area.

"That's a Spooky," Kevin said.

"Who told you?" I asked.

"I've read about them—modified C-130 cargo planes equipped with electric Gatling guns," he said.

In the dimming light, the faint drone of a prop-driven plane reminded me of a drive-in suspense thriller without the car speaker, while regular bursts of bright ribbons left no doubt that a "Spooky" circled on station.

"Every fifth round is a tracer bullet," Kevin said.

"Pouring lead on them like pissing on ants," I said, feeling somewhat avenged for that rocket. Charlie was getting his comeuppance.

"Nothing for Charlie to do but burrow into the dirt or hide in one of those caves," Paul said.

"Damn, I'd hate to be down there," I said, then yelled, "Eat shit," relieved that Spooky had creamed Charlie and not us.

* * *

The next day in the office Steve appeared, as excited as a kid with an orange cream swirl. "Hey, I've been released for out-processing."

I'd expected my closest buddy from Two Corps get-go would leave soon, but the news caught me off guard anyway. The office would become less lively, more of a dungeon.

Steve made the rounds for handshakes and well wishes.

I offered a hug when he came to me. "Take care of yourself, man."

"Yeah, you too."

"Write down your address for me, Steve."

"Look me up your first chance," he said as he handed me his address.

"Sure thing."

Once he'd left the office, everyone grew quiet. All of us were just that much closer to home.

* * *

Routines in my day-to-day activities smoothed the ruffles of inconsistency. On the other hand, boredom weighed on me and, along with the tide of my hormones, jockeyed for my attention. My fantasies of hot, rabbit sex with Pam, and contented lounges in bed afterward with gentle talk of love and plans together, eased the relentless weight of reality. And mail from "the World" continued to provide temporary escapes.

Back on our bunks for a rest after work, Paul said to me, "I heard we're having fireworks tonight."

"Wouldn't want to miss that," Kevin piped up from his cubicle.

"What exactly?" I asked.

"Can't say for sure. I overheard several officers talking when I left the office," Paul said.

"Oh, that's right, tomorrow is Tet, Vietnamese New Year," I said. "Count me in." TV images of Tet fighting two years earlier flashed through my mind, vivid as ever. *Charlie planning another shit-sandwich for us?*

* * *

"Shake a leg," Paul yelled from our barrack roof. "Fifteen minutes."

I clambered up and claimed a spot next to Paul.

News had spread. Guys sat or stood on barracks dotted around, while others milled about on the ground. Our roof provided a perfect place to lie back and study the clear, moonless sky. I couldn't recognize one constellation from another. Wished I could. I had never taken the time to memorize them. My field jacket, a replacement of my first, helped cut the chill from the cool, humid air blown by a whisper of wind. Light from the air base and Pie Slice created a sharp contrast to the darkness outside the perimeter.

"What time do you have, Paul?" I asked.

"Eleven … fifty-eight."

"Any minute," I said.

"Rock 'n' roll," Kevin piped in.

Except for low chatter from the small gatherings, everything was quiet, like a junkyard dog asleep. But no such thing as "normal" in 'Nam.

One minute passed. Another passed. Another.

Pop! Pop! Pop! Flares, shot high into the sky, illuminated everything for two hundred yards to our west.

No silhouettes of Charlie.

From our side of the perimeter, small arms and machine guns fired into the air. Tracer bullets marked the spew of hot metal threads that arced beyond the reach of our flares into the still blackness. Now, the junkyard dog, awakened and with teeth bared, foamed at the mouth and barked full force in a "mad minute," with lead blasted by everyone with a weapon.

Hoots, hollers, and whistles filled the air.

"Awesome," Kevin squealed.

Pop! Pop! More brilliant tiny suns swayed and drifted under their parachutes.

"Light 'em up," I said, our show a Fourth of July fireworks display. Except I knew those fireworks were coming from weapons made to kill.

We had another "mad minute" of firing, no break. Then, another. *Pop! Pop! Pop!*

After nearly five minutes the gunfire trailed off into sporadic bursts for several more minutes before everything grew quiet. And when the last flares burned out, everything beyond the perimeter road grew dark again.

'Nam could be that way: loud, aggressive, and deadly one moment, and peacefully calm the next.

Some higher-up must've ordered that. Our way of saying, Hey, Charlie, you won't surprise us this time. For sure, a wanton waste of ammo, but a chance to blow off frustration and show our firepower. Made us feel superior or safer, I guessed, but whether it demoralized Charlie or prevented an attack, I had no idea.

I climbed into my bunk. *How long will things remain calm?*

* * *

Late the next evening, our unit CO ordered us to formation next to our Detachment Headquarters. "This is not a drill," he started. "We're expecting an attack tonight. We'll issue each of you a helmet, an M-14, and ammunition."

After we fell out of formation and were issued weapons and helmets, Paul, Kevin, and I clustered together.

"Serious shit," I said.

"You three." Top pointed at us, motioned to a hole in the ground. "Man that trench."

No room for discussion. Top meant business.

Other personnel in our unit got parceled out and were assigned to specific locations dispersed over a wide area.

"Lock and load your weapons," our CO ordered. Those words, repeated by others lower in our detachment's command, rippled out like waves over the ranks.

Next to Kevin in the trench, another pea in our pod, I said with a glance, "No grab-ass. This isn't the time for shit-silliness."

"Like I'd want to," he snarled.

I'd wondered in Basic what type of weapon I'd handle in 'Nam. Couldn't envision I wouldn't, even when not a grunt, but guard duty had required I be issued an M-14.

In Basic, Drill Sergeant had lifted an M-14. "Pay attention, ladies," he started. "This is not your gun. This is your weapon." He grabbed his crotch. "This," he hefted his hand several times, "is your gun."

My platoon barrack mates had chuckled.

Drill Sergeant had interrupted them. "You need to know your weapon," he'd barked. "Repeat this: take care of your weapon and your weapon will take care of you."

We mouthed the mantra.

"Again!" he yelled. "You'd best remember this."

How could I forget?

A week later, Drill Sergeant showed us an M-16. "Most of you will carry these in 'Nam. You don't want to use a stick or rock to defend yourself in a firefight. If this weapon gets submerged … dirt or mud … dunk it … pretty sturdy … jams, eject the round … still doesn't fire … find a clean surface."

Our company's drill instructors mentioned 'Nam daily, wouldn't leave it alone.

On several occasions and despite my truck-driving qualifications, I'd joined my platoon mates—most destined for grunt-hood—on some marches to and from firing ranges. I locked and loaded both M-14s and M-16s, then shot at targets at different distances and from different positions.

"Imagine those targets out there are gooks," drill instructors had encouraged us. "Fire those weapons," they'd yell along the firing-range line. They'd wanted us primed to kill at a moment's notice, no questions asked, unlike the care Dad had wanted me to take with his 4-10 shotgun during squirrel and rabbit hunts after I'd turned thirteen.

But now, standing in a trench and facing our perimeter, I wasn't on the hunt for a small animal; I had to be ready to fend off Charlie.

No trees or hooches blocked our views along the road, out past the perimeter. Well out of yelling range, I'd seen farmers working their water buffaloes in rice paddies during the day. I scanned my section of the chain-link fence topped by concertina wire, thirty yards out to my front, and the dust-covered gravel road running parallel, illuminated by pale-yellow lights on poles. Beyond, there was nothing but black. *Charlie in the paddies?*

Every unlit place by our buildings and light poles inside the wire allowed apparitions opportunity to hide. *Charlie lurking there?*

I had no reason to believe Charlie could've already snuck inside our perimeter without our knowing, but I didn't put it past him, so I scanned those areas, too.

"Hey, Paul" I said, looking past Kevin who stood between us in the eight-foot trench. "You still cover Nha Trang. What've you heard about this?"

"A rumor floated around today. I didn't catch any details," Paul said.

"We're mushrooms, fed bullshit and kept in the dark," Kevin mumbled.

"Kevin, the fungus," I said.

"You're one to talk."

"Quiet, guys," Paul said.

Finger near the trigger, I rested my weapon on a sandbag at the front edge of our chest-deep trench, aware of the strong smell of dirt. I watched for a grenade lobbed over the wire, waiting for Charlie to charge across the gravel road, screaming words designed to rattle me into a frozen state. I listened for anyone to yell the words, Dinks in the wire! *Who knew how we'd react?* Untested in combat, we'd need to defend ourselves if Charlie attacked along our perimeter. And we knew Charlie could attempt infiltration and create havoc among us. I studied the fence out in front of me for signs of a sapper.

Part of me wanted to hunker into the trench corner. I figured Kevin and Paul wanted the same. "This is no time for beauty rest, guys. We shouldn't let our guard down." Not ready to die, I prepared myself to kill and rehearsed a confusing, up-close, life-draining-away-in-front-of-me struggle of wills and survival.

"If an attack comes, could you pull the trigger?" Kevin asked Paul and me.

"Yeah, don't want to, but I could," Paul said.

"I could do it," I said. I had enough anger about the army and 'Nam to chew wood. "All I need is a legit excuse to let it rip." I'd focus everything on Charlie. Unleash my rage—be glad for it and get thanked, not reprimanded. I could defend myself. I'd defend my buddy, Paul. Hell … I'd even defend Kevin, though wouldn't admit that to him.

"Me, too," Kevin said. "They'd deserve what they got."

The minutes dragged by. An hour passed.

"Damn, my legs ache," I said. My eyes, glued open, burned.

"Lean against the back wall," Paul suggested.

"Good idea," Kevin said.

I scanned for any motion, looking for anything out of place. Watched my breath rise in the dank air.

Another hour passed.

From behind us, a stone's throw away, Top yelled, "All clear." That command echoed around the Pie Slice.

I eased my finger off the trigger guard and flexed my hand several times. "About time. I'm beat."

"I'm ready for some shut-eye," Kevin said.

"Abandon your positions," Top yelled. "Clear your weapons and take them to your bunks. We'll collect them in the morning."

Weapon in one hand, I slouched back to my bunk.

With the laces loosened, I pulled off one boot while Paul did the same at his bunk. "How do you figure that, Paul? Our CO running us through a readiness exercise?"

Paul worked on his other boot. "I expect we had some reliable intel."

"You think we encouraged Charlie to change plans?" I removed my other boot.

"Never know."

Somebody in another cubicle farted.

Someone else yelled, "Need any butt-wipe?"

I fell back on my bunk in my fatigues and managed a fitful rest until reveille.

55th Military Intelligence Detachment members practiced live fire south of Nha Trang. (Hon Tre Island, in the background, lies about four miles distance and across the Nha Trang Bay in the South China Sea. I did not know what prompted that exercise, but suspected it was army SOP to maintain our proficiency. And that was the only time I fired a weapon in 'Nam.)

A view north toward Nha Trang. (Rice paddies and farm fields occupied areas on the left and westward. With its distinctive shape, the Pie Slice, slightly left of center, occupied an area adjacent to other military facilities and Vietnamese houses farther east. The airport runway lay on the right, with downtown Nha Trang beyond. The white Buddha statue occupied a distant hilltop on the right side.)

JELLYBEAN?

Kevin returned to the office from Detachment Headquarters in a cheery mood. "Mail call," he said.

Brought out of my study of reports and photos of the caves in the mountainside several miles from our western perimeter, I said, "No Katyusha today? Get a naked photo from your girlfriend, did you?" I asked.

"Wouldn't you like to know?" he snapped. "Maybe I got naked photos of your sister."

"I don't have a sister, but watch it, you may still get your mouth washed out with soap," I replied.

Kevin pitched an envelope on my desk. "You got one," he said.

I looked it over. From AIT Alex. I hadn't expected a letter from him … nor anyone else in 'Nam.

Hey, Connard,
Remember me? Alex from AIT?

Of course.

I hadn't bothered to keep track of anyone from Basic or AIT. Hadn't bothered to keep track of high school or college mates, either. Dad had moved us around enough times as I grew up that I'd learned to float along on the current of life's river, and considered most relationships scenery along the bank.

I decided to look you up, so I ran down your assignment records.

Maybe my records at Military Assistance Command, Vietnam, in Saigon?

I'll get to the point. I thought you'd want to hear about Jellybean. You remember Jellybean?

Soft-spoken, red-haired, light-complexioned Jellybean? How could I forget?

He died last week from a gunshot wound to the head.

Wait! What? I reread that sentence.

He died … gunshot wound to the head.

No! Mild, meek Jellybean? Dead? Jellybean at Holabird AIT, shit-silly after a few slugs of sloe gin, another casualty of 'Nam? Returned to the States in a body bag? Part of an anonymous newscast statistic? Not anonymous to me. Shot? Who shot him? I continued reading.

Shot himself while cleaning his weapon. They reported it as an accident, "… from a gunshot wound sustained while cleaning his weapon."

Shot himself by accident? No way, no how.
We'd all learned the proper way to clean a weapon in Basic. Always removed the clip and cleared the chamber first. No reason to believe anyone had issued Jellybean a pistol, an officer's weapon, so I pictured him cleaning an M-14 or M-16 rifle.
Accident how? No. Couldn't be. As hard as it was to face, I knew he must have done it on purpose. I read on.

Sorry to give you the bad news. Anyway, stay in touch. Look me up if you get to Saigon. I'm at Three Corps Headquarters.

With a quick calculation I determined that Jellybean, "shipped in" the same time as me, had lasted eight months. I tired to drop it there, didn't want to think about my time left in-country and the possibility I'd get stuffed into a body bag, too. Mute the rest of the morning, I wrestled with that bite of 'Nam shit-sandwich.

Alex's news embedded itself in me like a sliver of bamboo under my fingernail, and with no way to remove that splinter of 'Nam reality, it remained impossible to ignore.

That evening in my bunk, I responded to Alex.

Yeah, I remember you, Wade, and Jellybean. Could never forget our silly shit in AIT. Sad news, hard to believe Jellybean's dead. Thanks for telling me. Sure, I'll let you know if I'm coming to Saigon. Would be good to see you again.

Stay in touch, man.

Jellybean had been shipped home in a body bag as a result of an unseen enemy within. What the hell had he been going through to do that?

OFF TO SEE THE WIZARD

Qualified for R&R after my first thirty days in-country, I'd saved mine for a rainy day. Eight months in, plus a few days—and after the recent news of Jellybean—an emotional monsoon threatened to drown me. I would've puked up 'Nam, the loneliness, and constant reminders of death if I could've.

John had schooled those of us in the office on the R&R approval process before he left for "the World." He told us the requests bypassed the usual chain of command, which guaranteed approval upon request, except for the limitation of wait lists. Out of the loop, my CO couldn't block, deny, or rescind mine. It was the one time that I knew of when I could figuratively flip my finger at my higher-ups. Well, that, and going on sick call. R&R amounted to a seven-day 'Nam escape, and could mean "Rest and recreation, relaxation, recuperation, or rehabilitation." I'd opt, as I suspect a fair number of GIs did, for the more recreational aspect with plentiful sex, alcohol, and rock 'n' roll ... maybe even drugs, if available. Side orders of sightseeing and shopping could get crammed in but weren't essential.

"Where should I go on R&R?" I asked no one in particular. "Hawaii?" I pictured the palms and long, silky hair blown by gentle breezes that I'd savored on my trip to 'Nam.

"Married guys go to Hawaii to meet their wives. Single guys have little chance for Hawaii," Elliot responded.

I dismissed the idea of meeting Pam in Hawaii. "Well ... what about Australia?"

John had reported about his good times there with single, voluptuous, English-speaking Aussie women (who, according to my imagination, roved bikini-clad on the beaches in herds). My fantasy, driven by rumors, mushroomed beyond reality for sure ... but hell, that didn't matter to me, Mr. Pussy-on-the-Brain.

"The wait is fourteen months long," Elliot responded. "Everybody wants to go there. Most of those who travel there have extended for second tours."

"Another year in 'Nam to go 'Down Under'? Bullshit."

"You don't need to like it," Elliot said. "I'm just telling you like it is."

How many miracles had the universe, or any greater power, bestowed upon me—if any? Surgery at the age of thirteen to remove my nearly ruptured appendix and the week of antibiotics in the hospital afterward? Did that count as one or two? The Katyusha rocket that had continued over me and hit the fuel tank? One? I didn't know. For sure, if miracles existed, I wouldn't wait for one to go "Down Under." Wouldn't take the risk and lose my R&R. With my rutting season in full swing, I wanted I&I: intoxication and intercourse. And any woman with the correct parts—and not Vietnamese—would do.

My priorities? First: get out of 'Nam, as fast as possible. Second: avoid reminders of 'Nam. Third: uh ... well, there wasn't one. "No way. What other options do I have?"

"You can get to Thailand right away," Elliot said.

Another Asian jungle destination, though free of VC, seemed a remake of 'Nam. I shook my head. "Nah, not that interested in Thailand."

"Japan's easy. Hardly any wait, a week or two."

Japan presented a possibility. Modern, not as good as Hawaii and Australia, but better than Thailand. It offered an escape from the relentless swelter, jungle stink, and mosquitoes.

"I think I'll go to Japan," Paul said.

"Hey, Paul, I've got an idea," I said. "How about going together?"

Not a bad idea.

"Okay," he said.

All right, a wingman. Japan, I'm on my way. Patch me up ... no, fix me.

I knew no one could remove 'Nam from me like the doc had done with my ingrown toenail at Holabird, but I hoped to forget 'Nam, the suffering and hardship, and the loneliness of missing most everything back home. I wanted to get on with my life—really dream of a future, not merely hope for one. I wanted free love. Wanted to feel normal and not look over my shoulder every second.

* * *

Paul and I together, our R&R had started well.

On our descent into Tokyo, I watched the silhouette of Mount Fuji slide by beyond a window on the far side of the plane.

Inside the terminal, the cool air, the clean floors, and busy, well-dressed people who moved about with purpose, suggested no slouching. We'd been directed toward kiosks where friendly, young Japanese girls hawked guided tours and encouraged a browse of their literature, printed in English.

"Let's see," I said to Paul. "Stay in Tokyo?"

Faced with choices, I'd hardly had time to absorb the fact that I'd arrived in Japan, where the young girls were well-dressed and, better yet, spoke English, though not perfectly. At least I could have an understandable conversation with them.

I examined the possibilities listed in one brochure. "Quite a few options here. All designed for one-week 'Nam fugitives, I suppose."

Paul flipped through another of the shiny brochures. "I'd rather get away from Tokyo and see more of Japan." He offered me a different brochure.

"I wouldn't mind that. Tokyo's crowded. I'm not interested in any World War II crap, either. I don't need any reminders of war."

"Tour temples and shrines?" Paul asked.

"Nah, religion's the last thing on my mind."

"Japanese women?" he asked.

"First chance," I said.

He pointed to the brochure he'd handed me. "I like that trip to the World's Fair in Osaka."

"Hmm. The price looks right," I said.

We dug military script from our pockets, counted out the amount, and forked it over.

The girls smiled, pleased with our purchases. "Wait here. A tour representative will come soon to take you to a bus," one said with a cheery voice.

Couldn't help myself. *Would be nice to feel every inch of your body and explode inside you until I went limp all over.*

A minute or two passed before another young Japanese woman approached. Sporting a tour company badge on her dark-blue coat, she carried herself upright and looked straight ahead without reservations.

I glanced at Paul and said, "All right, on our way." I watched the girl's breasts bounce underneath her white blouse and switched my focus to her face before my interest became obvious to her and awkward for me.

"I am your tour guide. Please, follow me," she said in singsong English with a big smile.

Close behind, I watched her ass sway, and on the verge of creaming my pants, caught a sweet fragrance of delicate flowers. *Oh, mama.*

She led us to where several buses waited and pointed to one. "Your bus. Board, please. We will leave shortly."

My thoughts were like a bullhorn, *Yes, board you ... please.*

Paul and I settled into separate padded reclining seats among other GIs who'd already planted their asses. Everyone spread out from habit, I supposed. Welcomed by the smell of fresh leather, I picked a seat by a window. No need to interact with a guy who could fill the seat next to me, I'd feign sleep or watch the scenery.

Right on schedule, our bus, partially filled with GIs—easily identified by our short hair and khakis, and no doubt off the same plane—pulled out of its bay and headed for Osaka, where I could enjoy the bliss of pussy and booze.

I let my mind wander, wanting to rest and take things as they came, not worrying about the next second. No hassles—I wanted no hassles. I felt entitled to that after eight months of 'Nam shit, even longer of army crap.

City buildings and concrete canyons gave way to houses and open spaces with trees, all shrouded in varying degrees of darkness in the night.

I occupied my seat as though I suffered a bad hangover after a bender. In the dawn light, I fought off drooping eyelids and the urge to sleep. I gazed at the coastline, where waves crashed against a rugged shore and trees grew, scattered by nature in that random yet perfect way. A religious shrine subtly punctuated the scene. *No question, better than 'Nam.*

Prompted by those unmistakable sounds of a microphone, *Crackle! Clunk! Tap, tap!* I looked up to see our tour guide.

"Good morning," she said. "Now that you have had sleep, I will tell you about your tour. First, I want to pass around this microphone. Please, introduce yourselves."

Good morning? My eyes burned from the lack of shut-eye.

The mic worked its way to me.

"My name is ... " blah, blah, blah, "I'll try anything," I said, my subtle invitation for drugs issued to anyone listening.

* * *

As arranged by the tour company, Paul and I occupied an Osaka hotel room within walking distance of the World's Fair.

I looked out the window, about a dozen stories up, at distant views of the city. Traffic and pedestrians moved along the busy street below. Metro trains ran at regular intervals on elevated tracks and reminded me of childhood toys. Neon signs blazed, blinking their unintelligible scribble. A low overcast—a blanket thrown over the city, threatened to settle onto it. *Cold, anonymous, impersonal.*

* * *

In our khakis and equipped with cameras, Paul and I wandered around the World's Fair.

"Let's head into the Soviet Pavilion," Paul said.

To our surprise, the Japanese ushers waved us straight to the entrance, ahead of a long waiting line.

A few steps inside the entrance, a rush of childhood enthusiasm overcame me. "Ooh. Hey, Paul." I guided his attention to the space capsule that hung from the ceiling. "Look at that. Must be Yuri Gagarin's jalopy."

A tease, the Soviets were showing off without revealing any hardware secrets. Given the chance, though, I'd have examined that spacecraft in minute detail. I might've been tempted to volunteer for one of their space missions, if that would've gotten me out of 'Nam and the army. On the other hand, I likened the Soviets to plumbers and we Americans to watchmakers. They built crude, heavy, and clunky. We built refined, complex, and redundant. Finesse was our forte. We used specially designed pens for writing in low gravity; they used pencils.

I couldn't help but lay eyes on a red-haired, fair-skinned girl, dressed in a dark, two-piece suit, who stood in front of us only several feet away. *Nice.* My eyes feasted on her breasts hidden beneath a white blouse. *Her name? What would the army think if I talked to her? That I planned an act of treason or defection? What the hell?* "Paul, I studied Russian for two years in high school. I haven't kept it up, but let's see if I can talk with her."

She appeared to concentrate on someone or something across the room.

In my best formal Russian, I said, "Hello, how are you?"

Though close enough that she could hear me whisper, she didn't budge, remaining stone-faced.

Well, Katyusha, you stuck-up bitch!

I guessed my short-cropped hair, trimmed mustache, and U.S. khakis created some kind of Soviet-girl turnoff. But more likely, she'd been warned of an all-expenses-paid trip to a Siberian gulag if she talked to an American GI.

∗   ∗   ∗

The tour company had treated our GI group to an evening at a geisha nightclub.

"Begin with warm sake." The geisha's petite ruby-red lips moved in the chalk-white sea of her facial make-up. "One or two cups."

I turned to the guys on both sides of me. "Bottoms up and all that shit." The first small, sweet cupful went down smoothly. I requested a second and that went down smoother.

"Then, we switch to cold sake," she said.

The raw taste of room-temperature rice wine burned its way past my tongue and tonsils, then clawed its way down my esophagus before attacking my stomach lining.

"You can have more if you want," she offered.

"Yeah, sure," I said, and held out my cup. By that point, I didn't give a damn about the burn.

The gaggle of geisha around the room plied us with drinks, before one moved into the middle of the room, laid two pillows on the mat, and asked for a volunteer to participate in a game.

Not sure what she meant, I raised my hand.

She stood on one pillow and said, "You stand on the other."

About half-looped and the pillow no friend to my balance, I wobbled.

"Now we bump until one falls off," she said and gave my ass a tap with hers.

A friendly game of bump-ass! I deflected and evaded her direct hits, and in short order got into the spirit of competition. I wouldn't go down easy.

She upped her game. So did I.

Though I eventually succumbed, I suspected she ended up bruised and wondered, *What's with that American GI?*

* * *

Paul had gone to the hotel bar for drinks, but I wanted a different experience and had stayed in our room to summon a call girl. A phone call to order pizza delivery in New York City would've been more complicated.

"You called for me?" A Japanese female, not quite my height and a little older, stared at me with dark eyes.

I'd anticipated a knock at my hotel room door, but not that fixed gaze and hard voice. "Yeah." I didn't know what to expect. No one had provided me rules.

She entered the room and got straight to the point. "You pay me first," she said with the warmth and charm of a shark.

Despite my misgivings about her demeanor, I forked over the demanded moolah.

Clothes off, she lay flat on her back before I could remove my shoes. She offered a blank expression, avoided eye contact, and said nothing. For all I knew, she occupied herself with thoughts about painful constipation or death from some parasitic disease.

I made a sincere effort to climax in the presence of her indifferent display, but the harder I tried, the further away it got. Never a problem before, I knew her demeanor didn't help any. *What's up with that dead fish? I may as well try screwing an electrical wall socket.*

Embarrassed and out of breath, I said, "I can't do it. I need to take a break."

She sprang to life and snapped, "I can't help you then." She hurried to pull on her jeans and loose-fitting blouse. She slipped her shoes on in quick succession. Her underwear snagged by one hand, and her handbag clutched tight in the other with my money inside, she moved swiftly in one fluid motion.

Paralyzed by frustration and surprised by her comment, I watched.

Slam! She'd disappeared through the doorway.

That's not how I'd pictured my R&R when I'd discussed it in my Two Corps Headquarters office in Nha Trang three weeks earlier.

The call girl gone with a handful of my MPCs, and my time in Osaka nearing an end, I sat naked on the edge of the bed, alone and stunned. *What the hell happened? Track her down? Grab her by the neck and suggest a refund?* It dawned on me that I had needed that act of physical intimacy for more than just sex.

I stared across the room and through the window at the cold scene of Osaka. Jellybean dead, John gone Stateside, Rudy and Steve, too … all like pieces of me shed away. Even my mental pictures of Pam and Mom seemed dim and faded. I couldn't have felt any lonelier than at that moment. A flush of rage condensed into an urge. Like a movie or a vivid dream … I imagined myself taking a few steps across the room, crashing through the window, and plunging to the street below. *What the fuck? Where did that come from?*

I froze, afraid to stand, afraid my legs would carry me to that bloody fate. I didn't move. Didn't fucking dare move. All I could manage was an ass-plant on the bed. Seemed forever before that urge subsided.

Though relieved when it subsided, I wondered, *What was that? Where did it go? Will it return? Can I trust myself?*

I'd worked hard to protect myself from others' rage, including Charlie's—though not that well at times, I knew—but protect myself from me? *A drink … in the bar … on the first floor. Good idea.*

Clothes on and out of the room in a flash, I resolved to keep the whole episode quiet and not tell Paul … not tell anyone. *Well, for damn sure, Dorothy ain't in Kansas anymore.*

Looking back, as much as that experience nearly tipped me over the edge, I wonder what that Japanese prostitute must have suffered to become that numb. Was it her way of coping with an impossible situation? But at what cost? And me, I certainly hadn't been making the best decisions, seeking sexual comfort from prostitutes who were likely only there for survival.

* * *

Escape from that Osaka hotel room on my mind, I watched landscapes of neat, cultivated fields and lush groves, and small towns with immaculate, miniaturized houses and cars, speed by as our high-speed train headed north, back toward the airport near Tokyo.

Glad to leave Japan, I welcomed a return to 'Nam. I never believed I would've thought that, but in 'Nam I'd be farther away from those events in the hotel room. I preferred to think that experience and those feelings were part of that Osaka hotel room and not me, but I knew better. I hoped that distance from Osaka would weaken them, at least. Wanted to keep those feelings secret, never face them again … including my shame of them. The unsettling intensity of that call-girl experience and my subsequent suicidal thoughts made me aware of a darker, uglier side I'd never faced before.

As I look back, I wonder how that experience triggered my suicidal thoughts. It may have been that she touched a shame so deep in me that I turned my anger toward her onto myself. Regardless, the intensity of my anger and thoughts of suicide, and the deeper sense of being rejected, would subsequently take me years to put into proper perspective.

YOUR ATTENTION, PLEASE

"On another R&R, Hogan?" Elliot asked.

Caught off guard and back from Japan for several days, I said, "No, no."

"You got that report done on the history of 235th VC Battalion?"

"About done." I didn't need him riding me about that. Didn't need anybody riding me about anything.

I'd grown interested in reading the past info on the 235th and formulating a history report. The army wanted me to provide an opinion. That's what I considered an analyst ought to do.

I remembered Rudy's words: "You'll need to write weekly and monthly reports that include summaries of intelligence information in your section. Give them to John to review. He'll pass them to Lieutenant Raines for approval before they're sent on. Your reports become part of a broader summary that goes to MACV in Saigon."

Information in those reports ended up in the lonely bowels of the Pentagon, classified and buried among perhaps millions of papers— destined to become fossilized treasures for unborn historians or archaeologists, as far as I knew ... or cared. Or maybe they went up in smoke, destroyed by an E-4 in a MACV burn cage.

The 235th, decimated several times, lived on as a skeleton of its original self, I concluded. Charlie had clung to the name. The US Army clung to unit names, too. Banners, insignias, and citations hung on the walls of every unit headquarters I'd seen. Unit names preserved, campaigns and heroism remembered. *Oorah. Win one for the Gipper, and all that shit.*

Within the hour I handed my report to Elliot. "Here you go."

"Hey, listen to this." Kevin held up an intel report. "It's about a female VC commander who got wounded. Yada yada yada. Oh, here." He read an excerpt aloud: '… her left breast blown off in the fierce attack.'"

Guffaws erupted around the room. Though nothing about 'Nam was funny, no way I could contain myself.

Not "any" attack … but a "fierce" one. I pictured artillery and mortar rounds crisscrossing the sky, hurling dirt and shrapnel in loud explosions; radios barking situation reports and commands; adrenaline-filled combatants carrying out assigned duties, working to stay alive and killing their adversary; and frantic civilians seeking safety and anonymity.

But as the laughter died down, I considered: *Her left breast? A softer part of her humanity. Torn away and replaced by a bloody, gaping wound.* Another example of the brutality of 'Nam, where trauma was being inflicted every moment of every day. In secret, I acknowledged her commitment and sacrifice to a cause, though contrary to mine. *Damn, blown off!*

* * *

That evening after dinner, I showered and watched *Marooned* at the Pie Slice theater.

Fitting: they were stranded on the moon … I'm stranded in 'Nam.

By the time I hit the rack, the late evening hour suggested that most GIs had settled into their bunks. Not sleepy, I read my latest copy of *Playboy* magazine for a little peace and quiet.

BOOM!!!

"What the hell?" I yelled. *Incoming or outgoing?*

BOOM!!!

Another concussive wave slammed my face and chest—a momentary pressure, short and heavy, that violated my body. I'd rather have faced the wall of speakers at the Woodstock concert. Undetermined things, scattered throughout the barrack, rattled in protest.

"Outgoing from a one-five-five or a one-seven-five," Ray shouted back from the next barrack.

BOOM!!!

I hadn't seen or heard artillery pieces roll in. Knew from my model-building kid days that self-propelled one-fifty-five artillery cannon drove around on tank chassis. Bigger and heavier still, the massive and powerful one-seventy-fives put their smaller cousins, the fifty-fives, to shame. "The five-fives are wimps compared with these motherfuckers," I said to Paul, who lay propped up on one elbow in his bunk.

BOOM!!!

My mosquito net waved. Loose wood joints creaked and moaned. Dust, dislodged from rafters, rained onto everything. *The next blast throw me out of bed?*

BOOM!!!

I lost my cool. "Where is that thing? Right outside our barrack?" Up to a cross-legged sitting position, I said, "How much longer with this crap?"

No doubt, scared grunts in a firefight in the bush out there prayed for those rounds to hurry up.

BOOM!!!

"The last session lasted about ten minutes," Ray replied.

"I never heard these things from the Compound," I said to Paul.

"You had to listen for them," Paul said.

BOOM!!!

193

Several minutes passed before I heard Ray's muffled voice, as if wads of cotton plugged my ears. "It's over."

"I hope so." I couldn't fall asleep until my ears stopped ringing.

MOVE IT

"Hogan, you can move into the E-5 barrack," Top informed me. *Mistake? Or Top hinting at promotion orders for me?*

Regardless, I didn't want to jinx my luck and I sure wasn't going to challenge Top. His news helped push aside the nagging weariness of the slow passage of time over the past ten months.

Many GIs started their short-timer's countdown when they hit double digits. Not me. I expected I'd leave 'Nam at the end of my three-sixty-five at the latest and that time wouldn't move any faster to please me. I wanted to avoid reminders of my days left in-country. Wanted to avoid getting so depressed that I'd crack like Uncle Tunney … or Jellybean. A single glance at a report or calendar, and *Bam!*, my ongoing tug-of-war between hope and dread would be in my face.

I hightailed it to my bunk and broke the news to Paul. "I'm moving into an E-5 barrack."

"Okay, see you later." He didn't bother to look up from his magazine.

I'd hoped for more enthusiasm but understood his reaction. "Yeah. See you around."

* * *

Vincent passed me in the hallway of the E-5 quarters on the way to his cubbyhole next door. A five o'clock shadow stood out against his blotchy, oil-shine skin.

195

"Hey, Vincent, I'm moving in. Looks like we'll be neighbors."

Vincent, an easygoing guy off a farm in the Midwest, had gotten a promotion before our relocation from headquarters compound and had gone straight into E-5 housing.

"Good for you," Vincent said. "Promoted to E-5."

"No, not promoted yet. Got my fingers crossed, though. Top gave me word to move in."

"Great. Let's get a drink later."

"Detachment bar?" I asked.

"Yeah."

I took stock of my new digs. Another example of rank's privileges, an E-5 cubicle would provide me privacy. Though smaller than Lieutenant Cullins' room, my cozy quarters would be safer … in a way. I calculated the odds of getting hit by a mortar round close to nil. Charlie would've had to put one in my lap. *Best not get cocky; stranger shit happens.*

I personalized my space with a thoughtful selection of a new batch of *Playboy* and *Penthouse* photos and my favorite poster from the Moody Blues.

* * *

Drink in hand, Vincent occupied a stool at our detachment bar when I entered.

I grabbed the seat next to him and ordered a vodka tonic. I said to him, "Not the watery crap in the Enlisted Men's Club at Corps HQ."

"After this, I'm going to find some tail," he said. "You interested?"

My attention riveted by his comment, I said, "Yeah, where?" I took a swallow of my fresh, chilled drink, assured that the detachment-made ice wouldn't give me the runs.

"Front gate."

"News to me. Opportunity to do bad things with women? Tell me more." I took another swallow.

"You can escort indigenous into the Pie Slice, when you want," he said. "Drink up and let's go together."

"Count me in."

Vincent and I, dressed in our wrinkled fatigues after our day's work, hot-footed to the guard gate, then looked over the eager line of hopefuls decked out in their colorful plumage.

"You like, GI?" all those in the queue asked in succession when I made eye contact.

Vincent glanced back, one specimen in tow. "Enjoy."

"Break a leg, dude."

I shopped until I found a suitable bird, one who showed promise of life, unlike that dead fish in Japan, and escorted her back to my private sanctuary, where I believed my perspective on GI life would improve.

* * *

Less than a week later, I reclined on my new bunk after work and read my latest copy of *Penthouse* in earnest.

Knock, knock!

"Who the hell?" I mumbled and made my way to the door.

A guy, clad in fatigues with E-5 insignias and a sheepish grin, stood in the hallway. "Top says you got to move. This is going to be my room."

Had I heard that cherry right? "What are you talking about?"

"You need to go talk to Top."

Didn't my in-country time count for something? Besides, "possession is nine-tenths" and all that shit.

I dredged up every ounce of indignation I could muster on my way to find out what was going on. "Top, an FNG at my door says I have to move out of my room."

"Yeah … that's right," he said without hesitation.

"But Top, you gave me word to move my stuff in just a few days ago."

"There's nothing I can do about it. You'll have to move." Not a flicker of sympathy. Top's expression didn't change.

The fickle finger shoved up my ass, I steamed over my version of slow-motion musical barracks, exiled back to the E-4 commune. I dropped a trail of choice words on my way back to the barracks to collect my gear, not caring who heard. "Damn it … son of a bitch … fucking bastard."

That FNG, about to occupy my recently acquired living quarters, gloated at the doorway as I completed packing. *No way to settle the score without getting busted.*

Primed to explode over every injustice done to me, I glared at him the last time I left the room, tempted to give him a belt and rearrange his jaw. "Not funny, not fucking funny," I said with my last bit of self-restraint.

Dejected, I returned to the E-4 barrack, where my old bunk waited. I'd moved nearer the officers, again … and likely the next mortar attack.

Kevin approached with what appeared a smirk. "Mama-san told me somebody took her shoe polish."

"So," I said, "what've I got to do with that?"

"It's up to you as head E-4," he raised one eyebrow, "to talk to her about it."

"Well, don't do me any fucking favors, Kevin." I paused a moment before adding, "And wipe that silly-ass grin off your face."

The seniority of rank in the barrack fell on me, which meant the responsibility for fixing problems there—some problems damn near missions impossible. There never seemed to be a shortage of jealous bloodsucking leeches (Kevin, for example) to crawl out of the woodwork with 20/20 hindsight and unsolicited advice and dump shit on me.

* * *

Next morning, I asked, "What's wrong, Mama-san?"

She pointed to a bunk in the back corner of the barrack. "GI take shoe polish. He no give back to me."

Always empty before, I noticed that a green-wool army blanket covered the mattress. A pillow in a white case occupied one end and a mosquito net draped the whole bunk, though I saw no one nearby.

Another newbie, no doubt. Anything like the FNG who'd taken my private E-5 room? The piss-perp at in-processing or the field-jacket thief? Or any of the assholes I'd encountered in Basic?

"Okay, I'll talk to him," I told Mama-san.

* * *

After work and back in the barrack, I noticed a guy in the corner cubicle I'd not seen before.

Yep, another cherry. I took a deep breath and approached, not sure how to start. *Stay calm.*

"Hey," I said to him with a nod.

"Hey," he echoed and rubbed his upper body with an army-green towel.

"Mama-san says that her shoe polish went missing. She left it around your bunk. Do you know where it is?"

"You calling me a thief?" he growled.

Whoa.

The low-cut sleeveless undershirt that he pulled on accentuated his upper-body strength. More muscular than me … and taller, he had me by fifty … sixty pounds, easy.

Armed with Mama-san's comments and no one or nothing else to back me up, I said, "No, but Mama-san says she left her shoe polish in your area. Do you know where it is?"

He smeared deodorant under his arms. "I don't know where her damn shoe polish is."

Mama-san's goods held hostage inside your locker? Try as I did, my stolen glances failed to penetrate the metal locker door. *Open the door to look? Best not.*

No idea what melodrama he'd play out, and no wish to have him wipe the floor with my ass, I eighty-sixed the idea of further confrontation. "Well, if you find her shoe polish, let me know." *Cheapskate motherfucker!*

No response from him except a quiet stare that made me want to run away and, at the same time, jump square into his shit. *If your life depended on me, you might not make it. Probably not, anyway.* But I turned and walked away. *Tag him and bag him.*

* * *

The next day, I broke the news.

"Mama-san, I understand you think he took your shoe polish, but I couldn't get it back and don't know where it is." Unsure how much she understood, I shook my head. "No shoe polish."

Her usual smile absent, face taut, she responded with a string of Vietnamese words.

Of course, I didn't understand what she said but caught her drift. Theft of her shoe polish was a significant hit to her earnings. Poorer than us, she could ill afford another supply out of pocket.

Obligated—at least, in my mind—to remedy Mama-san's problem, I offered her money. "Buy more shoe polish." With a hand motion toward my area, I said, "Use my bunk if you want. Okay?" I shook my head and pointed toward the corner. "Don't leave your things there."

She caught my drift.

I regretted my inability to return her polish, which was what I considered the proper resolution to her complaint. But, with that shit-interaction added to my collection bag of grievances, one more nail was driven into my notion of our collective American purity of purpose and moral superiority.

YOU LIKE, GI?

Several days after my eviction, I crossed paths with my former neighbor. "Hey, Vincent, did you know I got kicked out of the E-5 barrack?" I said.

"No. Why?"

My body tightened. "Top moved in an E-5 FNG."

"Damn, that's too bad." Vincent's face appeared covered in a layer of sweat or oil, difficult to tell which.

"A fucking 'ninety-day wonder.' I've got nowhere to get laid without peepers and catcalls. I'd get more privacy in a bunker than in my bunk, but still, I—"

"Want to use my room?" he said.

"Yeah, man. Thanks. I appreciate that. How about tonight?"

"Sure. When?"

"Seven?" I said.

"Okay, I'll steer clear for an hour. Probably hang out in the bar or take in the movie."

The big hand on the seven, sharp, I cruised the working-girl employment line outside the Pie Slice entrance gate and found a suitable painted-and-perfumed specimen. Then I hauled her to Vincent's room.

* * *

The next morning I checked to see why I itched and tingled.

"Jesus H, what the hell?" Hand-sized patches of red, oozing blisters covered my upper legs, lower back, and private parts. "FUCK!"

Straight to sick call, Doc delivered his verdict. "You have a case of herpes," he said. "Not curable, but manageable. The pustules will ooze but disappear after a few days. I'll give you some cream to put on them. Otherwise, keep them dry and don't scratch them."

Where had I gotten it? That prostitute? Vincent's bunk? How could anyone not know, or worse, not give a shit? I had a hard time believing I'd gotten my case of herpes from Vincent's bedsheet, so I blamed the prostitute.

* * *

That evening I eagle-eyed the lineup of suspects at the gate, though at a short distance away to avoid the need to talk to any of them personally. They stared at me, as I did them.

Wearing a wig? Hiding behind heavy makeup? I hadn't memorized her face. Unable to identify the culprit, I walked away without the satisfaction of a good yell. *Her next victim? Some other unlucky bastard.*

I resolved to be more careful in my choices of sexual partners, though I wasn't sure how to go about that, exactly.

Not sure what to say to Vincent, I didn't bring up the subject. He made no mention, either. But I wondered if he had contracted herpes, too.

Over time I came to realize, as Jimmy Buffet says in his song "Margaritaville," that my case of herpes was, well ... "my own damn fault."

MARBLED OZ

"Jellybean bunked there," Alex told me and pointed.

A tight, dark-green wool blanket covered the lower bunk, no doubt occupied by a cherry not long after Jellybean got shipped home. Quiet, we stood a moment and I stared while images of Jellybean's fair skin, thin frame, and soft voice came to mind.

Earlier that mid-May morning, eleven months in, I'd accompanied Gaston to the Three Corps Compound in Saigon. *Me, big shit, in Saigon with the major on official business.* Gaston being involved in briefings, I figured, gave me the go-ahead to do my own thing. *Maybe Gaston isn't all bad.* I hadn't gotten the full picture of the reason for the trip, or where we were in the military food chain. I didn't care, but escape from my work desk provided me a welcome break from my humdrum routine.

I'd followed Alex's directions, straight for his barrack. We saw each other right away in the open bay of double bunks, and after a brief hug, started our talk about Jellybean, who'd been gone several months.

"Suicide?" I asked.

"Couldn't handle all the pressure here, I guess," Alex said. "By himself at the time, I never saw it coming. Would've done anything if I'd known."

"I can't believe he's dead."

"Me, neither."

I had to ask, "Where'd he do it?"

"On his bunk but I didn't see anything," Alex said. "They'd removed him before I got here."

Silence engulfed us in the otherwise empty barrack.

Not sure what to say, I tried not to dwell on my images of Jellybean's act, instead picturing him back at AIT, shit-silly after a few swigs of sloe gin. I achieved mixed results, while I pickled in the brine of the whole fucked-up thing. No need for a lengthy discussion. No way to bring Jellybean back. Also nothing to prevent Alex or me from doing the same shit ... not really.

Alex motioned toward the door. "Let me show you around our compound."

Relieved to experience a change of scenery, we stood behind the barrack, several steps from a tiny finger of a river—more like a ditch or open sewer drain. Trash and bits of vegetation floated on the brown water that sloshed at the bank.

My bout with an ingrown toenail in mind, I said, "I wouldn't dip my big toe in that."

Alex pointed off to our right. "That's the Mekong River," he said. "VC operate freely at times over there."

"Damn, in Saigon, too?" I said. *Charlie's eyes on us from a hidden vantage in those reeds on the opposite bank?*

"Not a problem for me," Alex said.

"Perfect cover. Kind of close, though. A hundred yards on a football field always seemed a long way to me. Across this river ... not that far."

"Want to get lunch in the city?" Alex asked. "I know a good place."

Unsure but encouraged by his calm attitude, I opted for some distraction. "Okay, let's do that."

* * *

Alex and I sucked on chilled beers, chatted, and enjoyed plates of steamed rice mixed with vegetables and beef, soaking in the multi-colored atmosphere in the restaurant while recorded Vietnamese music played in the background.

"By the way, where did Wade end up?" I asked.

"Four Corps, the Delta. We've exchanged a few letters, but I haven't seen him since we left AIT."

"I've had no contact with him," I said. That's where we dropped our conversation about Wade. He'd remained on the periphery of friendships for me, though I'd spent as much time with him as Alex and Jellybean.

Alex finished his second beer. "Let's catch a pedicab rickshaw."

"That'll work for me." I drained the last of my second bottle of suds. "I've never ridden in one of those."

Our sinewy driver, dressed in a dingy white short-sleeve shirt and shorts, was happy to earn a few bucks in military currency. He cranked the pedals as he wove us through the tangled, trash-littered Saigon streets, which I considered an overgrown version of Nha Trang. Conical hats and ugly-plaid short-sleeve shirts moved about as their pedestrian owners headed in every direction. Bicycles and horn-honking motorbikes jockeyed to pass in the free-for-all traffic. Derelict buildings lined the congested streets, crisscrossed overhead by a chaotic mesh of electrical wiring. Everything screamed out as a noisy, tense, sprawling heap of humanity in a desperate scurry for survival.

With a flash, drawn back to reality, I realized Alex and I were helpless. We had no way to defend ourselves from an attack. *I'll scream, turn away, or close my eyes if one comes. Not dignified, but at least it will be short and quick ... probably.*

Our driver turned a corner, taking us past a row of makeshift cardboard hovels.

Without expecting Alex to respond, I ranted, "That's disgusting. People live this way? What the hell are we fighting for? Those are hardly big enough to provide shade from the sun or cover from a sprinkle, much less a monsoon downpour."

"War refugees live there," Alex said. "Most of those people migrated into Saigon from the countryside. Want to see the American embassy?"

"Yeah," I said. "I remember newscasts of the fighting there during the Tet Offensive." Those images had been seared into a prominent fold of my brain.

We pulled into a crowded roundabout, the center dominated by a large bronze statue of a South Vietnamese soldier.

"Let's get out here." Alex pointed. "The embassy's not far down the street."

I motioned toward the statue. "What a joke."

"How so?" Alex responded.

"You know Charlie's scared to death of ROK soldiers—respects those tough South Korean bastards. Shows us respect, too, because our technology kicks his ass. But he holds the South Vietnamese soldiers in contempt. He understands they rely on us to bail them out."

"You're not very hopeful."

"No. On their own, the ARVN fold like wet cardboard."

Not far down the busy street, a large white building came into view.

"There's the American embassy." Alex pointed at about the same time I spotted a large American flag waving above the rooftop.

Surrounded by a manicured lawn with scattered shrubbery and enclosed by an eight-foot metal grate fence, the white-marbled fortress gleamed in the full sun, in contrast to the dinginess of most everything in 'Nam—a vision of power and influence, a version of the Emerald City of Oz.

Surprisingly, a gush of patriotism warmed me, like a vodka shot sliding down my throat, despite my misgivings over much of what we were doing in Vietnam.

Two armed ARVN guards outside the main entrance gate appeared relaxed, in contrast to their counterparts inside the metal grate fence. There, all pomp and precision, marines in red-striped dress blues and white caps paced defined routes inside the perimeter, while others stood frozen at scattered posts.

Vehicles and pedestrians hurried along the street and paid no attention to those inside the compound.

A lone car pulled up to the gate. One guard approached and talked to the driver while another guard examined the car's undercarriage with a mirror on the end of a pole. After the second finished his inspection and nodded, the first guard opened the gate.

"That looked easy." I thought a moment. "I wonder if they'd let us in."

"I don't think so, but I've never tried."

"On second thought, probably not. We're peons." *What had given me that idea?*

* * *

Upon my return to work in the office at Two Corps Headquarters, Elliot looked up from some paperwork in his hands. "Good news, Hogan. A batch of new promotions came in and you've gotten yours."

I adjusted my stool. "How wonderful," I mumbled. *Won't help me much in 'Nam, but maybe I'll eat less shit Stateside?*

"A big operation started down in Three Corps," Ray said. "We've crossed into Cambodia."

My attention was suddenly riveted on him, along with everyone else's in the office. "What you got there, Ray?"

"The newest issue of *Newsweek*."

I noticed the corners of its pages quiver.

Kevin blurted, "We should've done that sooner."

Never without an opinion.

"Where, Ray?" Paul asked.

"A place called the 'Fishhook.' A storage complex. They're finding huge caches of weapons, but there's very little fighting. The army considers the operation classified."

"We get better information from magazines than from the army," Kevin piped up.

Duh. That's nothing new. I looked at Kevin. "You think?"

"It's big news back in the States," Ray added.

"Pass that over to me when you're done with it, Ray."

Kevin added two more cents. "We're mushrooms, kept in the dark and fed bullshit."

"Yeah, we got it, Kevin," I said. *You're full of it, for sure.*

Raines had stepped out of the office for a latrine break.

"Let's check the radio," Elliot said.

We listened for a few minutes, but Armed Forces Radio said nothing about Cambodia.

"You guys ever heard Hanoi Hanna?" Elliot asked.

"No," Ray said.

Elliot checked around the room. The rest of us shook our heads.

"We're not authorized, but it probably wouldn't hurt to listen in, briefly, just so you recognize her spiel," Elliot said and dialed to a female voice that ranted in heavy-accented English. "That's her," he said.

She encouraged American soldiers and ARVN to defect to the wonderful workers' paradise in the north and not support the aggressor American president.

What crap!

"Okay, now you know," Elliot said and switched off the radio before Raines returned.

Who did she ever convince? Not me, babe.

209

A makeshift shelter in Saigon, which appeared abandoned. (While in a rickshaw, I passed a cluster of huts, likely built by refugees from the countryside.)

KEEP THEM DOGGIES ROLLIN'

First thing in the office that morning, Raines announced, "I want two volunteers to take our jeep down to Cam Ranh today." He looked at me. "Take a couple of hours and catch a chopper back this afternoon."

Me?

Near the start of my twelfth-month in-country, I considered myself in the home stretch. Simple ticks on a calendar had started my countdown chart at thirty-five and a wake-up, but I didn't dare get my hopes too high. Maybe, just maybe … I'd avoid a body bag.

Raines never said much in the office. Didn't need to. Gave marching orders to Elliot and allowed him leeway in running the place. He read or wrote reports at his desk in a corner next to the windows, out of my line of sight. When the lieutenant talked, we listened. Raines, a lowly second Looie, could still put our asses in a sling if he wanted.

I didn't know who'd dreamed it up or how the conversation began, but about two months earlier, we rotated coverage of provinces in Two Corps, which wasn't a bad way to reduce the tedium. Coverage of Khanh Hoa Province, which encompassed Nha Trang and Cam Ranh, fell into my lap. None of us owned a given area in Two Corps, and the military machine could replace us in a hot minute, like interchangeable parts or little weenies in a can. Though I knew the army didn't want to replace any of us, they had to. GIs rotated out daily, their one-year tours completed, while others went back to the States in body bags.

Raines maintained a steady gaze on me.

Volun-told. Cornered, with no way out. I had no compelling retort or excuse to shift the outcome. I doubted my quiet office mates, heads down and suddenly busy, wanted to go. And if I refused, Raines could order me outright. Boredom and peer pressure finished icing the cake. "I'll go, sir." *Fuck me.* I could only hope, at least, that higher-ups were exercising good judgment and thought the jeep delivery reasonable enough not to casually send me on a one-way trip to my demise. *Weren't they?* I hadn't seen or heard reports of any major activity in our area for a couple of weeks.

"He'll need a second man," Raines said to the others in our office.

I figured I'd make the most of an iffy situation and attempted to pitch the idea to Paul or Ray. "Another chance to get out of Nha Trang," I said as I looked at each in turn.

"I'll go, sir," Kevin said.

Wonderful, fucking wonderful. Alone, in a jeep, me and Loudmouth for who knows how long?

"I got shotgun," I said, grabbing our M-1 and shoving in our one clip of ammo.

"Don't chamber a round till you're out of the building," Raines ordered.

He'd catch hell from the general if I fired our weapon inside the Hotel, and I'd get even worse. "Yes, sir." No killing spree inside the Hotel in mind—I figured Raines considered I'd let a round loose by mistake. I collected all of the loose ammo we had in the office, which might buy an additional twenty seconds in a lead sling-fest if I rationed them.

As Kevin and I headed down the hallway, I hefted the weapon several times and without a look at him, said, "Peashooter. Nothing to write home about. At twelve I owned a BB gun this big."

Kevin remained quiet. I figured he hadn't heard me, but no matter.

At the jeep, I said, "Okay, Kevin, no fancy shit. Don't stop for anything as long as the engine runs and the vehicle moves. Not for a piss, not for photos, not to trade off driving. And drive like hell, if we encounter Charlie."

"I agree, no stopping," he said.

No back talk? No wise-ass quip? I slid into the passenger seat. "We're covered. I won't hesitate to use this thing." At the ready with a round chambered, I rested the M-1 in my lap. "This crate gassed up?" I asked.

"Yeah, it's full. Did you see the Pie Slice movie last night?"

"No, didn't catch it," I said, annoyed he wanted to chitchat. "Just pay attention to your driving, Kevin." *Shut him up awhile?*

"On the rag today?"

"Never you mind."

We set off for our forty-mile delivery mission to Cam Ranh Bay, like two nervous Chihuahuas in an open tin can—vulnerable yet determined to scream and bluff, despite our frailty. Focused on the road ahead, as well as to the right and left for possible dangers, I suspected everything: people, dogs, birds on the wing—even trees along the road. I'd long accepted Charlie's ingenuity and cunning, and knew that Charlie dreamed up creative shit for jeeps on roads to cause American casualties. He played hide-and-seek well. Deliberate, sneaky, with no uniform or badge, he bobbed and weaved among the civilian population.

Why is that woman in black silk pajamas staring at us? "Keep driving, dude," I said with my eyes glued on her until we'd passed her by.

West, out of Nha Trang for twenty minutes, we approached a T-junction stop sign at Highway 1, South Vietnam's main north-south road. Northwest of the mountains that created our sunsets from the

Pie Slice, we'd flanked the position where Charlie likely fired that fucking Katyusha rocket at me and we'd dropped bombs. According to the information I'd seen, the same area had caves that we'd strafed, and was where grunts had been sent on search-and-destroy missions, all to clear Charlie out.

I spotted the stop sign fifty yards ahead. "Turn left. That'll take us south."

"Yeah, I figured that out," Kevin quipped.

I harbored no doubt Charlie moved on cat's paws and damn near hid between two pieces of paper. "Keep it rolling, dude. Don't stop."

"Not by the hair on your chinny-chin-chin." Kevin hit the gas from a rolling stop.

The smooth, fresh-paved road ran straight and flat.

Good.

The engine and tires generated a steady hum, a constant white noise.

Good.

I scanned the terrain—scenic countryside of unattended, cultivated fields and scattered trees with an occasional shrine or hut. I wanted to enjoy the view. Couldn't. Knew an unannounced bullet from a stationary sniper or from another vehicle could strike us down without warning.

Is the guy leading the water buffalo, Charlie?

The road ahead remained clear.

Good.

The white noise remained steady, suggesting no engine problem or flat tire.

Good.

I kept an eye on a dog patrolling the road.

Another mile behind us means one less to go. Is that kid by the side of the road Charlie?

We'd traveled south awhile, and passed the mountains on our left.

"Getting close," I said. My hope and prayer, rather than a certainty.

"I gathered that."

We neared the next junction, evidenced by the sign that pointed left: CAM RANH BAY.

"We just might avoid a boogie with Charlie," I said.

An urge to inhale a stiff drink came over me when we passed the gate onto the base. *How did Charlie miss his golden opportunity?*

I lapsed into a moment of distraction and pictured sending new letters to Mom and Pam when Kevin pulled our jeep up to the drop-off point.

Today I rode to Cam Ranh Bay with a guy from my office to deliver a jeep. Can't stand him. I rode in the passenger seat with our office peashooter in my lap and wondered if a VC sniper would shoot us. Our peashooter wouldn't have helped us much, even if I'd used it.

No ... change that.

Today, I traveled to Cam Ranh Bay to deliver a jeep. Saw scenic countryside along the way.

Lord knew Mom thought up plenty to worry about on her own. She didn't need my 'Nam blow-by-blow, nor did Pam, so I parceled out my 'Nam experiences only on a need-to-know basis.

* * *

Our jeep-delivery mission accomplished, Kevin and I hitched a ride back to Nha Trang from the same graveled chopper pad I'd visited months before.

After our jackhammer kidney massage and when clear of the turning rotors once our chopper had settled onto the airbase tarmac, I said to Kevin, "I bet that's the best sex you've ever had."

He sneered. "You'll never know."

DUST IN THE RAFTERS

"Hey, Connard, I've cleaned the top of the rafters over my bunk," Kevin yelled. "Come take a look."

Encouraged by his enthusiasm, I considered that maybe I wouldn't face mutiny during our barrack pre-inspection cleanup and face a repeat of that piss-in-the-corner FNG at Long Binh in-processing. Just three days after Kevin and I delivered that jeep to Cam Ranh and neck deep in the shit-news of our upcoming inspection, I yelled back, "I'm looking at the bunker. Give me a few minutes."

"Don't you think you ought to take a look before I continue?" Kevin said.

"No. Sounds like a good idea to me. Go ahead."

After Paul had followed me outside, I stepped down into our assigned bunker for a better look while he remained at the entrance.

"There's trash in here," I said to Paul.

I heard Kevin's voice again. "I want you to take a look before I continue."

"What's his fucking problem?" I half-whispered to Paul without expecting an answer. I yelled back to Kevin, "That's not necessary. If you think it's a good idea, go ahead."

"Would you clean out the trash and tidy up the bunker?" I asked Paul and climbed out of the bunker.

I'd no sooner straightened up than Kevin met me face-to-face and started his barrage. "Why don't you want to check out what I've done? Don't appreciate my work? I could do a better job overseeing this cleanup. Think you're better than me?"

What crawled up your ass? After more than enough of Kevin's dumb-ass insistence and ready to cold-cock him, but not sure if he'd take a swing at me, I said, "Paul, would you hold him?"

Kevin didn't resist Paul; instead, he smirked.

The situation under control, I hoped that would give me a moment to think and Kevin an opportunity to cool off.

But Kevin continued, "Yeah, that's right. Get somebody else involved."

Without thinking, I reached out and touched Kevin on the chest. "You need to settle down."

"Oh, have Paul hold me so you can take a sucker punch," he snarled.

And at that moment, I knew I'd fucked up. "Let him go, Paul. I'm sorry I got you involved, man."

Kevin was primed for a fight, no doubt, long before our interchange had started. My teeth and fist clenched, I wanted to knock his nose out of joint. I was just figuring I'd whip his ass good, when in that one pause between breaths, I noticed in my peripheral vision a jeep cruise across the street intersection not far away. The driver was checking us out.

In that instant, I knew I verged on behavior that would lead to a disciplinary Article 15. Our CO held the authority to bust me in rank, take my pay, or give me any number of punishments he dreamed up. I didn't want to go back to the States as an E-4 or worse. By instinct, I ducked back, out of the jeep's line of sight.

Jaw unclenched, spit shot from my mouth as I growled in a low voice and pointed at Kevin. "You want to get busted, you stupid shit?" I backed away. "Don't you dare follow me!"

Ray sat on his bunk in the adjacent barrack, not ten feet away from the whole episode. He'd heard everything. His furrowed brow and ghost-pale color made that clear.

"Son of a bitch. I let that fucker get to me," I told Ray and hoped Kevin didn't hear me and re-escalate. "Less than thirty days to go and I don't need his shit."

Disappointed, I blamed myself for not avoiding that escalation, another near miss of a brawl. I should've remembered the red flag Kevin waved when he'd told me about his high school football stint.

By the time I returned to my bunk, I didn't give a rat's ass whether Kevin had cleaned the rafters or not. Regardless of army repercussions, I knew I was capable of popping Kevin even if he did nothing else.

And dust in the rafters didn't make a fart-in-a-hurricane difference; nobody bothered to look.

I posed at the front entrance of my E-4 Pie Slice barrack near the end of my one-year 'Nam tour.

DROP IN THE BUCKET

"How much time you got left?" Kevin asked me. Caught off guard, I figured that was a taunt. *Brought that up to bullshit or take a cheap shot at me?* On my shit list, I didn't want to talk with him and didn't expect he'd talk to me.

Most of us knew how to shuffle papers and bullshit at the same time. As long as we wrote our reports and showed up on time, Raines didn't care about an occasional low-key comment. But we knew not to draw attention from passers-by in the outer office, which would get him into a bind with higher-ups.

"Twenty-two and a wake-up, but I don't want to talk about it."

"Ooh," Kevin said.

"Ahh." Paul grinned.

Two-cent comments thrown around the room started the ribbing I'd anticipated. Hell, everybody caught a dose of that when their time came, and nobody forgot about it for long. Our banter blew off steam and we practiced that ritual like baseball players wearing dirty underwear, hoping to continue a winning streak.

Kevin grinned. "You got that short-timer's attitude yet?"

A good omen for him—if I make it out, he can, too. "Trying to avoid that," I said. I didn't want to get cocky, let down my guard, and make a rookie mistake.

"Lighten up, you'll make it," Paul said.

"Easy for you to say," I replied. "I'm hoping for a drop, maybe a few days off for good behavior."

"Aren't we all?" Kevin asked.

"Don't jinx me, damn it," I said.

What bizarre shit. I expected boasting could lead to my doom, piss off the universe, or tweak my karma, so I nurtured my attitude in private. Superstition and pessimism crawled into my bunk, ate next to me, showered with me, and looked back from the mirror. The shorter I got, the stronger they grew. Fate, karma, or whatever had brought me to that point, despite my ignorant behavior, and I didn't want to screw things up.

Should've guessed that would happen; superstition lurked in my family. Once, Dad had stopped our car in the street. "I'm not crossing the path of a black cat," he'd said and detoured us several blocks out of the way to get home.

And once, halfway toward the front door at my grandmother's house after a visit, Mom had stopped and asked, "Which way did we come in? We have to leave through the same door."

"Why?" I'd asked.

"Because it's bad luck otherwise," she'd said.

My twenty-one-year-old, science-oriented brain considered superstition a load of bunk, but I needed everything going in my favor, just in case.

Tempted to get religion, I considered prayer as a possible avenue to get a drop—military lingo for the standard-year tour, a three-sixty-four plus a "wake-up," decreased by a few days. Instead, I fondled my version of mental rosary beads. Rudy, whom I'd replaced, got a four-day drop, lucky bastard. Elliot got six days, lucky fucker. Steve got five days. Replaced a week ago, Raines hadn't talked of a drop in the office. Gaston must've extended, as he was still around, angling for a promotion to lieutenant colonel, no doubt.

Me? Will I be extremely lucky, somewhat lucky, or even a little lucky?

* * *

With another mark on my countdown calendar, I faced fifteen and a wake-up.

Kevin returned from Detachment Headquarters, the day's mail in hand. "A couple of you got important news." He tossed an official-looking envelope on my table. "For you." He handed one to Paul. "You got one, too."

I pulled out a set of orders and read them silently.

Report for out-processing ... thirty-day leave ... Fort Bragg.

My orders, the army's decision, was printed right there on paper, as flexible as hieroglyphs carved in stone. My drop had turned out to be a drop in the bucket. Me, not extremely lucky, not even somewhat lucky. Luck had played no part.

"How much drop did you get?" Paul asked.

"Two days." I held up two fingers held up for emphasis. "Can you believe it? Two lousy, fucking days." All my feelings about 'Nam rolled into a hairball, I would've coughed them up onto my table if I could've. I'd never considered extending for another tour in order to shorten my three-year commitment to the army. No way! Not a volunteer for 'Nam in the first place, I didn't want to spend an extra minute there. "Hey, Paul, your orders to leave?" I asked.

"Yeah. I'm leaving next month."

"Where're you going Stateside?"

"Baltimore." He remained straight-faced. "You?"

"North Carolina," I said, envious as all hell of his assignment. *Crap. Baltimore, closer to Pam, would've been perfect.*

Over the next days, my focus shifted toward "the World," and in my half-daze, I maintained a low profile.

* * *

"Well, guys, this is my last day in the office," I said. "I head to Cam Ranh in three days and I'm released from office duties to finish out-processing." I'd probably see most of them around the Hotel or Pie Slice, but in case I got too busy or … well, whatever. "Keep your heads down."

"Good luck," Ray offered.

"Yeah, you too," I told him.

Paul's eye twitched. "I'm right behind you."

"No promises of happy ever after," Kevin injected.

"No, and no promises to stay in touch," I shot back.

Most of us knew we'd never see each other again, wouldn't want to even if we had the chance. I'd do fine never to see or talk with Kevin again. Ray I liked, but we didn't exchange addresses, I don't know why. For sure, I wanted contact with Paul and got his address. A couple of weeks after Steve had left, I'd searched but couldn't find the address he'd given me. I regretted I had lost that.

* * *

Everything passed in a blur as I scurried around the compound from one item on my checklist to the next without a glitch.

When I exchanged my "funny money" for U.S. greenbacks, I considered I'd made progress. I hadn't touched the real stuff since I'd arrived in 'Nam, and had paid for everything in hard military currency.

A group of us who were out-processing gathered for instructions about sending our belongings home. A captain-in-charge started, "Each of you will receive a wooden shipping container. Pack all your personal items into your crate. Shipment will take about thirty days. Don't pack perishable food. You'll end up with a stinking mess if you do."

Wouldn't want that.

With the wag of an index finger, he continued, "No contraband allowed—no AKs, no grenades, no ammunition, no flammables, no drugs. If you do pack contraband and Customs checks your box, you'll end up in deep shit. They'll send your ass to Leavenworth."

Army prison? No way.

"Whatever you can fit in there will go. Weight's not an issue. Keep several changes of uniform in your duffle bag for transit."

The tangible items of my year in 'Nam in a crate didn't amount to much.

* * *

On my last scheduled full day in-country, and as one of a few dozen guys, I boarded a transport south out of Nha Trang. Every seat on the plane was occupied by a guy eager to escape 'Nam, the air heavy with the rot-smell of a sweaty jockstrap fermented inside a boy's gym locker.

I'd welcomed the monsoon rains in 'Nam for no other reason than they cleaned the air, washed away the ever-present reminder of decay, though the primeval stink had always returned with the sun.

* * *

Disembarked after our ride from Nha Trang with duffle bags in tow, we were herded together at the edge of the tarmac on a concrete basketball court, crowded together with not even room to dribble a ball. "You need to wait here until we board the plane," the captain said. It was the same guy who'd instructed me about packing my crate—no doubt outbound with us, too.

Twelve months gone by, I lived at the other end of my 'Nam tour. If a fickle finger didn't crawl up my rectum, I'd return home alive.

Visions of a new, exciting life of untold days ahead occupied me, though the army still owned my ass for another eighteen months.

The hour of our departure came ... and went.

"Where's the plane? What's going on?" several guys grumbled.

Fingers crossed that Charlie wouldn't lob mortar rounds at us, but otherwise bored out of my skull, I pondered all manner of bad shit. Over the past year, boredom and anxiety had risen and fallen in varied intensities one moment to the next—sometimes panic, generated by loud noises, dull thuds, the yell of "Incoming," as well as darkness, weapons carried in the open, and the proximity of razor wire.

The mix of fear and boredom I'd stewed in had started when I'd received my draft notice nineteen months earlier, a lifetime ago now. They'd become familiar companions whom I didn't care for.

The necessary permission granted, I relieved myself at the nearby latrine. Afterward, we marched a short distance in single-file to a mess hall for chow.

"Shit-on-a-shingle," a guy in line ahead of me complained when the hot, chipped beef with gravy plopped onto the toast already on his metal tray.

The greasy-spoon cook, tied to the kitchen for long hours from early morning to evening every day, responded, "Eat it, don't it eat, up to you."

Though nothing for a French chef to write home about, I wasn't that picky, and I ate without complaint. Whenever something looked unappetizing, I didn't put it on my plate or requested only a little. Afterward, I dumped what I didn't want.

After our meal in the mess, we were returned to the covered waiting area, where I stayed like a housefly on sticky paper.

Several more hours passed, damn near an eternity. At least we waited in the shade.

The captain appeared from a nearby building and apprised us of the situation. "Our plane's been delayed in Japan due to a mechanical problem. As soon as they complete repairs, it'll be on its way here."

I glanced at the guy next to me. "How about a different plane?" I said in a lowered voice.

"Don't go anywhere. You need to be ready to board when it arrives," the captain added, then walked away.

"The fucker," somebody grumbled. "He's probably been stretched out on a comfy bed in air conditioning,"

"Yeah, as if I'd wander off into the jungle," I said to the guy next to me, "or escape by sea with a swim to Japan or beyond in a mad fit, à la *Catch-22*."

"The usual shit. Hurry up and wait," the guy replied.

"I thought I'd be out of 'Nam by now," I grumbled. *Will I get out? 'Nam consumed Jellybean. Sent him home in a body bag, a casualty of "a gunshot wound sustained while cleaning his weapon." Accident? Yeah, right!*

The sunlight faded, replaced by the blue-tint hue of lighting from a lone pole near the captain's hideout.

Sprawled on the concrete pad, draped over our duffle bags, trapped, we resembled dead and wounded on a battlefield, cast in stark silhouette by a stationary flare.

My morale had been twisted into a knot. For more than the past year, a constant threat had weighed on me. I wanted to relax, not have one eye or ear on alert, and not wonder every second if I'd live through the next. A fickle finger—our delay—had forced me to chew another bite of 'Nam shit-sandwich, tested my ability to maintain ... and gave Charlie more time to fuck me over.

I wanted the thirty-day leave owed me. I wanted to see my family, to wallow in the smell of fresh-mowed grass, to feel ice on my forehead, and not wonder if a mortar round would punch through the ceiling while I slept. I wanted American pussy, wanted to grow my hair, not wear starched fatigues, and not need permission to take a piss. I settled in for a fitful rest. Had no other choice.

More hours passed by—another eternity amid snores, coughs, and ass scratches.

* * *

The sun rose. And there I'd remained, another day in Vietnam, another day I hadn't enjoyed. *My drop? Shriveled like a dick in cold water.*

The captain reappeared. "The plane's been repaired and is on its way."

"Hours away," I mumbled.

"Fucking army ... fucking 'Nam," somebody grumbled. "I'm burning my uniform when I get home."

Wide-spread bellyaching followed, with generous doses of confetti-tossed four-letter words.

The passing minutes created squandered hours. All the while I thought about how Charlie could screw me.

Another outgoing group assembled nearby.

A plane approached and landed. I joined a chorus of others with, "Yay, finally."

We watched the bright red-and-white paint and the clean, shiny aluminum shape come down the runway and taxi to a stop.

A single line of FNGs filed out the door and down the ramp. My mind flashed back to the words of warning from a year earlier: "If we encounter incoming rounds, keep moving until you're off the plane and get to a bunker or hit the deck." *Come to think of it, I see no bunkers.*

FNGs, fresh meat for the grinder, had no clue, and no way to know. Easy to spot the newbies. They wore their skittishness like their crisp, starched fatigues. I'd long since hidden mine behind a callous thickened by cycles of panic and boredom.

The other group filed toward the plane.

"What the hell?" I blurted.

"Bastards," one guy yelled.

"Assholes," someone barked.

"When are we getting out of here?" another said.

"Yeah," several others echoed.

The captain reappeared. "Settle down. We're all anxious to get out of here. It shouldn't be much longer."

"Easy for him to say," somebody murmured, "living in luxury while we're corralled."

"Wait. Hurry up and wait. That's the army's way," the guy next to me complained.

"You got that right," I replied.

That other group boarded the plane in front of us.

"Fuckers ripped us off," somebody muttered.

Their plane taxied to the runway. A scream threatened to force its way past my tonsils, tongue, and teeth. *Won't help.* The thick trail of black exhaust from the plane's engines as it climbed away confirmed that they'd gotten out.

* * *

Two more hours passed.

"I see a plane," someone shouted.

Everyone watched and fidgeted as the commercial jet landed, then taxied to a stop. Looked no different from the last plane.

Our captain reappeared. "That's us. Grab your gear and form up in a single file."

My "freedom bird," about to get me the hell away from 'Nam, pulled up within mere yards, and I didn't give a shit who heard me over the idling engines as I said, "Get me on that fucking thing."

Fatigue-clad guys filed out of the plane, down the ramp, and across the tarmac in a steady stream. They looked the same as the last group, not much different than little interchangeable sausages. *More FNGs ... about to learn what "the 'Nam" really means.*

When our turn came to board, no order or encouragement needed, I maintained my position in the single file across the tarmac, up the ramp, then down the aisle toward the rear of the plane. Each step carried me closer to home ... I hoped.

"Proceed to the last open row," our fellow captain said.

"Yeah, yeah. Blah, blah, blah. I got the drill," I whispered. *Will we get shot down?*

* * *

Our plane taxied.

We turned.

I willed the plane off the ground and away. That didn't work. I crossed my fingers. I reminded myself to breathe. *Wait. Hurry up ... and wait.*

We sat.

Sporadic yells that began to encourage us on filled the plane, then turned to a chant. "Let's go. Let's go. Let's go."

The engines roared, accelerating us down the runway.

None too soon.

Some guys clapped, some cheered, others whooped.

We lifted off.

Not much longer. Last chance, Charlie.

Individual voices mixed with the air moving about the cabin and joined an increasing chorus that built to a full-throated clamor.

I welcomed the blessed whir of retracting wheels.

Charlie had a dirty, last-second trick to pull?

I jockeyed for a view, watched the beach pass below us, and we climbed out over the South China Sea.

I took a deep breath and sighed. A quiet tear formed in my eye. *The plane could still crash but ... I survived 'Nam ... I survived 'Nam!*

"THE WORLD"

Thousands of feet above the Pacific, the guy next to me said, "When I get home, I'm burning my uniform."

"You don't know how many times I've wished I could do that," I said.

"I'm flushing my dog tags," another guy across the aisle added.

My ass chapped. I remained a wanted man. The army expected me to serve out my next eighteen months, the reckoning of my enlistment and assignment as an Intelligence Analyst. How would I get through that?

Before my Stateside duty at Fort Bragg in North Carolina, thirty days of freedom lay ahead as a reward for my stint in 'Nam. Not enough time, nowhere near enough. The army couldn't give me enough time off. I'd drive my new vitamin-K-orange, econo-car Plymouth Road Runner, which I'd ordered months earlier. I'd eat Mom's fried chicken and dumplings. I'd let my hair grow, shove my army issue into a closet, and kick around in my worn tennies. I had an endless list ... but my priority? Forget 'Nam.

* * *

Faced with onward flight choices from Sea-Tac, my first landfall back on the continent, I pondered several possibilities, though briefly. *Tour Seattle? Hell no. Home ... pronto.*

* * *

Mom, Dad, Verlon, and several aunts and uncles welcomed me at the terminal gate in Louisville's airport, Standiford Field.

One aunt asked first thing when we hugged, "How are you?"

"I'm okay," I said. *Am I?*

An uncle offered his hand and asked, "How was it over there?"

"Not too bad for me." *What a crock!* I couldn't even convince myself of that. Even though I hadn't seen combat directly, my experience hadn't been a cake walk. I knew I'd been changed, yet didn't know just how much or in what ways.

I had no simple answers for their questions, though provided them short-cut responses. Nothing of my overall experience had been that easy to comprehend and sort through, much less put into words. I had no way to explain 'Nam in terms they'd understand, not in the deepest way that I'd known it. I suspected no GI could.

Relieved to be away from 'Nam, my brain told me I didn't have to expect a rocket or mortar attack—didn't have to expect to hear someone scream the word, "Incoming." I saw clues all around me, from the clothes people wore to the absence of trash littering the floor. Everything appeared newer and brighter in color. I detected no heavy smells of mold or rot filling warm, humid air. Everyone spoke words I understood.

My bones told me otherwise, however. Nothing quite right; everything felt familiar, though different. Rather, everything reminded me of Vietnam, a queer reversal of the previous twelve months when I hadn't been able to avoid thoughts of home everywhere I looked—not from the presence of familiar things, but their absence.

Each day, I expected to hear orders barked in army lingo and the bugle calls of reveille and taps. When I sat down to eat, I noticed the absence of that inevitable background mess hall question, Where's the hot sauce?

Conditioned to react, as if I'd get shot or needed to seek cover at any moment, I found myself instead surrounded by a void of silence when in public. As if Vietnam and our GIs there didn't exist. As if my year meant nothing to those for whom I'd worn the uniform. All the while, however, protests and reports of our dead continued to occupy evening TV newscasts.

I encountered no welcoming committees, not that I was advertising. I received no speeches, got no recognition aside from my family, nor was I invited to join a confetti parade in New York City or in my neighborhood. I knew 'Nam vets didn't get hero treatment, unlike those from WWII. But the lack of public recognition, as if Vietnam was a secret most everyone preferred to sweep under a rug, left me to question my patriotism and why I'd reported for draft induction in the first place.

I'd done my patriotic duty, but understood I'd deluded myself about our common purpose. Clearly, the army and Vietnam had dissuaded me of my naïve notions. We Americans weren't special— we could and did engage in the same disgusting behaviors toward one another as everyone else around the world.

My short hair marked me as military-issue, and to avoid an ambush by the anti-war protesters, I maintained a low profile and slouched around. I avoided getting heckled and condemned, though I don't know how I managed to escape that.

Uneasy and unfulfilled, I discovered a little each day that nobody and nothing at home had changed during my absence. I realized the wonderful utopia I'd imagined didn't exist and that "the World" had never been perfect. Even my old Ford Fairlane occupied the driveway, second gear still busted. Instead, I'd changed ... and had conjured a make-believe homeland.

Loneliness filled my days. Sex-crazed and dissatisfied as ever, I hit the booze hard on weekend nights and cruised around town in my new wheels in a nonstop search for a *Playboy* centerfold to force herself upon me. The proximity of any young woman provoked my body to react with a hard-on at unpredictable times, and I guarded against the embarrassing moments when a stiffy bulged in my pants.

* * *

With a deep breath, I dialed the operator at the Pentagon, my mouth coated with paste and heart lodged in my throat. "I want to talk to the individual responsible for Intelligence Analyst assignments."

About two weeks Stateside, as the constant readiness to take cover at a moment's notice eased, the reality of Fort Bragg loomed. My focus shifted to survival of a different kind than in Vietnam, and a flicker of hope grew for reassignment to avoid my faraway North Carolina posting.

"Hold on, I'll connect you," a young female voice replied.

"Hello, Sergeant Higgins here," a male voice said.

"I'm calling to find out about changing my assignment," I started. At his request, I gave Higgins my details: name, rank, MOS, home town. Then I continued, "Several guys in my outfit got assignments closer to their homes. What're my options?"

"Where's your assignment?" Higgins asked.

"Fort Bragg, North Carolina."

"The only other openings available at the moment are in Fort Hood, Texas. Would you rather go there?"

Alex's words during AIT flashed across my mind. He'd told me that Satan had dreamed up Texas. *Shit.* "No," I said to Higgins. "I figure Fort Bragg is closer to Louisville and the weather isn't as hot."

"I try to get everybody as close to home as possible," he added.

235

How about the Pentagon, near Pam's doorstep? Nah, too much tight-ass military there. I'd wash out in a New York minute. "Okay, thanks," I told him. Why'd I say that? At least he'd listened and seemed sympathetic.

* * *

"Sir, Specialist Hogan reporting," I said.

The captain, my new company CO, looked to be in his mid-thirties.

My one-month leave at an end, I'd put off announcing my presence to him until Monday morning. I'd waited as long as I dared and had spent the previous night on the half-empty second floor in a nearby barrack on the QT.

"So, you're one of mine?" he said, his comment halfway between a question and a mouthwatering discovery.

You're not sure? Put me out of my misery.

That morning, I learned what I'd probably do for the remainder of my army stretch. About one hundred puke-green-fatigue-clad GIs reported to a large, open building built on a smooth concrete pad, with a metal I-beam frame and corrugated sheet-metal sides and roof. Neck-high partitions cordoned the interior space into walkways and smaller work areas.

My new workplace was a glorified stall in a barn, and I was one of the herd.

Second Looie Quinton, my new immediate work boss, near my age and with a pockmarked pink face, started my orientation. "Sit here. This will be your seat." He picked up a small chrome wheel with gauge and handle, then demonstrated the technique on the map laid on the table in front of me. "Measure the distance between road junctions," he said.

A quick study of the map told me all I needed about the place in question. A desert terrain in the Middle East. I noted topos covered three other tables worked over by busy-little-beaver GIs with my same rank. *A trained monkey can do this menial work. Hell ... I'm that trained monkey. And working in plain view of Second Looie with no place to hide or goof off.*

Quinton held up a blank form. "Record that information on these forms. Include road width and surface type as well," he said slowly in a soft-spoken voice, though I noticed a quiver.

"Then what, sir?"

He pointed to a table a few feet away. "Put your completed form in that box on my desk. I pass them on for someone to input the information into a computer database. When we're done, the army will be able to determine the most suitable and quickest routes between any two points at a moment's notice."

Higher-ups planning for another war? To get a better read on Quinton, I asked, "'Nam vet, sir?"

"Everyone here is a 'Nam vet, except for a few Civil Service management personnel tied to the project. They wear civvies and badges."

I liked Quinton immediately and considered him a good Joe. He didn't seem the type to dish out shit. I decided I'd try not to hold his rank against him or consider it a personal fault. Maybe I could think of his rank more like an unfortunate affliction.

Then, there was the heat. By late morning the midsummer sun worked its way through the building's uninsulated metal skin and stagnated our work-space air. With our cubicle floor fan at full blast, we crowded around in turns to cool off, encouraging dawdlers to move along with the words, Hey, don't Bogart the fan.

Still, I expected that "the barn" would be the easy, breezy part of my Bragg life. The biggie? I'd still need to endure a gauntlet of obsessive army regimentation, the spit-polished parts of Stateside duty I'd dreaded for months, meted out by my unit CO and Top. I'd face no rocket or mortar attacks; I wouldn't need to be on guard for snipers or sappers wanting to kill me. But daily army rituals, undiluted by Charlie's presence, would be a different kind of bad.

Get along and get out. No reason to believe most everyone else wasn't doing the same, aside from the lifers. But I'd avoid them the way I'd elude a plague. In the meantime, nothing and nobody could pull me out from behind my well-fortified wall topped with barbwire where I'd taken refuge. At least the army couldn't control that.

* * *

A week-and-a-half at Stalag Bragg, the shit-news came from Curt: "The fuckers want to do an inspection tomorrow."

"Shit, a revisit of Basic," I said.

"When?" Wayne asked. He bunked in my barrack's one downstairs private room. Burned out as a result of being in the army and Vietnam, I figured, he had that I-couldn't-give-a-shit-less attitude.

"At roll call," Curt said, his straight-slicked hair laid combed to one side. He bunked in the barrack's one upstairs private room and spent most of his time listening to music.

"What're they trying to pull?" Wayne asked.

"A bunch of shit," Jim grumbled in his Georgia twang. The dark mole on his left cheek looked penciled on. He bunked in the room with Wayne. Struck me as a joker.

The worst part of Stateside duty came to roost—the get-your-shit-squared-away-check-up-your-ass army way of doing things. And the CO and Top could bury us under a deeper pile of crap whenever they wanted. No matter how bad, my army life could always be made worse.

"I'm wearing my 'Nam brass," Wayne scoffed, meaning his Montagnard bracelet.

Most of us owned and wore one. Our signal to those in the know. Our version of a navy tat on the arm.

"Me, too," Jim seconded.

* * *

The next morning, Top ordered us to formation for roll call. Gave us a cursory exam. "I notice some of you are wearing bracelets," Top Sergeant said. "You aren't allowed to wear those. They're not part of your uniform."

Well, shit!

After formation, Curt watched me remove mine. "I'm not taking mine off," he said.

"Do they want a mutiny?" Jim asked.

Safety in numbers. I'll wear mine, too. But I hedged my bet and tucked it up and under my buttoned fatigue sleeve. *How are they gonna return us to our blissful ignorance now that we've seen 'Nam?*

* * *

A few days later, Top gave us another shit-news announcement during morning formation. "It's come to our attention that a few GIs frequent the coffeehouse in Fayetteville. Be advised, you're not allowed to go there."

What?

After formation, I heard someone ask him as I walked away, "How come, Top?"

"Subversive elements," he answered.

Subversive? A legal local coffeehouse? Afraid of free-minded people drinking coffee and appreciating music? Surely, not a den of VC or Russian spies. And higher-ups telling me what to do off base to boot? Bullshit.

* * *

That Friday evening, I exercised my modicum of free will and checked out the coffeehouse. Had to. I hadn't been there beforehand, but the injunction had acted as a personal challenge and also piqued my curiosity. Besides, maybe, I'd meet a woman!

The place was cozy. Big enough to hold eighty people, maybe. Didn't charge a cover. The army may have considered the joint a den of iniquity, or lair of spies, but I didn't care what the army thought. I claimed a seat, which faced a small stage. Then, Pete Seeger—the legend—occupied the stool on stage, right there in front of me within whisper distance, as he sang anti-war songs and shared his ideas, none of which were new to me.

Steeped in thick smells of guzzled coffee and stale beer, I followed along in my head, "*Where have all the flowers gone, long time passing. ...*"

Pete sang, "If I Had a Hammer," another familiar tune to which I knew the words.

Pete subversive? Nah. Who's-It in charge at Bragg is suffering a major disconnect.

Not critical of GIs or vets, Pete blamed our military and the president for our mess in Vietnam, and made no bones about that.

I followed along with his words, "*... waist deep in the Big Muddy and the big fool said to push on. ...*" That about nailed my sentiments of the last two years.

Despite my inclination to meet a suitable companion, I quickly learned that my appearance told the women in the coffeehouse, and in Fayetteville, all they cared to know. And, I learned they didn't want any part of a short-haired GI, the army, or Fort Bragg. Torn down the middle, I raged that they couldn't or didn't see me as an individual, a warm-bloodied, eager, good-looking male with a new car … but it was hard for me to blame them. I didn't want any part of short hair, the army, or Fort Bragg, either.

* * *

Saturday night on base, midway into another purgatory weekend, Wayne approached me with a mischievous grin. No way to hide his one broken front tooth, an eye magnet.

I pointed at his mouth. "What happened?"

He chuckled. "I got drunk and smashed my face on the barrack back-entrance steps last night. Jim and me use the back entrance because it's closest to our room. Anyway, want to smoke some good shit?"

As much subversion here as in any coffeehouse. "Sure. What the hell else is there to do?"

I wanted to go home every weekend, but couldn't wrap my head around a seven-hundred-seventy-mile drive to Louisville, then back, during a two-day weekend. Three-day weekends would be little more than a turnaround—an express-from-hell eleven-hour drive each way, at best. Those would hardly provide time for anything except eat, sleep, take a dump, and cruise a street or two looking for a loose woman. But Louisville, like Fayetteville, didn't offer up any easy women in my experience, either. I recognized that I was in a desperate, near-mad search for a willing woman on the off chance. I understood that I didn't know how to relate to them in a meaningful way. Nor had I built up the nerve to bring up sex to Pam, who lived only four hours away.

"Let's take a ride in my car," Wayne said. "We need to cool it with smoking in my room."

I'd already joined Wayne's weekend smoking circle in his two-bunk cubbyhole-room-turned-dope-den on the first floor. While smoke from our joints and clove cigarettes clogged the air, I made believe we were safe behind the closed door, though a "duty officer" could demand entry any minute.

Everyone in our barrack knew who smoked and who didn't. If they cared to know, they just needed to follow the scent or simply ask. Everybody would tell you straight-up yes or no, cut and dried, as long as you didn't yell it in the streets or blab to "the man."

Four of us piled into Wayne's car. Jim claimed shotgun. Curt and I took the backseat. Not far from the nearest parking lot, and in the darkness, Wayne eased his Pontiac sedan next to the barrack adjacent to ours and across from our front steps.

"Hey, that sign says no parking," Jim said.

"Yeah, you sure we should park here?" Curt asked.

Wayne stopped the car. "This'll be all right. That sign's just a suggestion."

Not the best of thinking in my mind, but no way I'd bail. Didn't want to spend the evening alone in the barrack.

Wayne rolled a joint and lit it.

The first pass encouraged me on my blissful way.

"Do you guys believe in ghosts?" Jim asked.

"No," Curt said. "What brought that up?"

"I can't stand our barrack. Thought I saw a ghost the other night," Jim replied.

What's going on with him?

Wayne giggled. "What's wrong with you, man? Too much dope?"

"Yeah, you been abusing?" I asked.

"No," Jim answered. "I use dope, but don't ab-use it."

We all roared.

"Yeah, Wayne, you're right." I passed the joint to Curt. "This weed is good shit."

Curt exhaled another drag. "That place gives me the creeps, too. You guys hear the second-floor creak? Dead giveaway for anything moving around after lights out."

I glanced around for a reconnoiter of our surroundings. "The whole thing is a déjà vu of Basic Training, except for all the empty bunks around."

None of us pressed each other for details on things, especially 'Nam. We observed the code: If anyone wanted you to know, they'd tell you.

With the car's windows rolled up, a cloud of burnt ganja filled the interior. And things were going fine until a flash of light appeared from behind us.

"We got company," Curt yelled.

I took a quick look. "Shit, we've been flanked and ambushed from the rear."

"Quick, throw this out." Wayne handed the baggie of weed to Jim. "And ditch the roach, too."

The overhead interior light came on and Jim pitched the offending herb under the adjacent barrack. And with that move, we'd defeated the purpose of the no-smoking policy between the barracks. Those WWII bone-dry wooden barracks threatened spontaneous combustion. And if that building caught fire, we'd have one big-ass bonfire that would take out our barrack and my neat, square-cornered blanket on my bunk in the process.

"Roll down the windows," Wayne said.

We exhaled and used our hands in an attempt to shoo away the evidence of our conduct.

The probing light stopped at Wayne's door. "I'm not sure what's going on here, but I smell dope," the guy growled.

The "duty officer," no doubt.

"You're not authorized to park here," he bellowed. And after a pause of breath, said, "Get out of that car."

Quiet, we stood, eyes squinted, while the guy grilled Wayne and blinded us with his flashlight.

After several minutes, he ordered all of us except Wayne, "Get out of here and don't come back."

Huh? I headed to the steps of my barrack, a good spit away. One foot on the first step, I caught myself. *Bad move, Bonehead.* I pivoted and hoped our inquisitor hadn't noticed. Then, I followed the others into the relative darkness for about thirty yards where we regrouped, out of the line of sight of Wayne's car.

"I can't believe he let us go," Jim said.

"Me either," I said.

* * *

Wayne filled us in the next day. "He's one of our company officers and is 'short.' Doesn't want to delay his discharge with paperwork or testimony."

"Escaped by the hairs on our chinny-chin-chins," I said.

* * *

With no contact since Nha Trang, I decided to write Paul a letter. I bitched and complained about the army. Clued him in on my situation.

We have some good weed here, dude ...

I waited for his response but none came.

After reflection, it dawned on me—at Fort Holabird, training ground for army spooks, hush-hush stuff—not that much into marijuana anyway, Paul wanted distance from drugs. And that meant distance from me, as well.

I didn't follow up and he became another friend gone by the wayside. First Rudy, then Steve, then Jellybean and Alex, Ray and Vincent, now Paul.

* * *

A few months later, during morning roll call, Top announced, "E-5s can qualify for an off-base housing allowance."

Live off base? Fucking A. Anywhere out of that barrack and not subject to unannounced inspection would suit me. Fingers crossed, I figured the army, aware that its kettle brimmed with malcontents at a rolling boil, wanted to disburse troublemakers and usher us on as fast as possible.

"Listen up," Top went on. "The following personnel have been approved for an off-base housing allowance." He consulted a list. "Blah, blah, blah ... Hogan ... blah, blah."

My ears lying?

With a mobile home about a mile beyond one of the base gates as my new digs, I let my contact with Wayne, Jim, Curt, and all the other guys in my barrack drop off, except for when I saw them in "the barn." Not to avoid them—I simply didn't want to hang around on base.

* * *

Bragg sweltered in the long days of Carolina sauna-summer months.

Pam and I had talked several times by phone. She remained at home with her parents and on several visits, I never planned things well enough to go "all the way." But even after all my experiences with prostitutes, I hadn't learned how to talk to a woman about sex. I'd let money talk for me.

"I know a place to get away for a weekend," Pam told me during a phone call not long before an upcoming Labor Day weekend.

"Sounds good," I replied. *Yeah, an opportunity to get down with Pam.* Every minute away from Bragg and the oppressive North Carolina heat would be additional bonuses.

245

"Meet me here and we'll go in my car," she said. "I'll arrange things."

* * *

Two weeks later, her hair tossed by the warm wind, Pam and I glided down the road in her red Opal convertible.

"Look at my new car," she'd beamed as we packed our luggage in the trunk.

Ocean City waited beyond the Chesapeake Bay Bridge. Everything seemed right in my world; that bridge and our trip could be a good omen. Would it be a dramatic turn for the better? Maybe an opportunity to crawl from under the oppressive weight of my last two years? Would it lead to a solid, ongoing relationship with Pam … beyond letters and phone calls?

Settled into a motel room, we got naked. What was there to discuss? Our effort, however, felt awkward, mechanical, and fumbling.

I'd expected fireworks of red, white, and blue. Instead, the fuse fizzled. Though we both came, I felt no explosions, nor did the earth move for me. Could that have been because we were both nervous? Or because she hadn't warned me of her period? I didn't know but blamed myself. I concluded that my anticipation, drawn out by my long year's wait in Vietnam and then some, had created an impossible expectation, at least for me. Once again, reality stepped on the fantasy I'd constructed, and that sucked big-time.

Although our talks together, the seafood meals, and strolls on the beach and boardwalk were as comfortable as a well-worn pair of shoes, questions, hesitation, and doubt distracted me. Not sure how to start or where it would lead, I didn't mention my disappointment over our sex together. I tried to refashion my perspective about the whole thing, but couldn't, and so gnawed on that piece of gristle.

* * *

I spied the young guy as I pulled my Road Runner up to my trailer.

He approached me with a smile. "Hi, I'm Brett," he said. "I rented the trailer next to you." Dressed in fatigues, eighteen, I guessed (near my brother's age), he sported a close-shaved head, blond mustache, and one gold earring.

I'd fled the barn first chance after another dog day, eager to ditch my sweaty fatigues and lounge on my couch in a blast of cold air straight from the air conditioner. "Come on in," I told him.

"I'm here for my mandatory one-month summer duty," Brett said. "I joined the National Guard to avoid the draft. I only report one weekend a month and one month each summer."

One month? Easy peasy. I could do that blindfolded. "What about your earring?"

"The fucking sergeant told me I have to remove it while on duty. I ain't taking off my ring," he said.

Spunk! The army hasn't beaten him down ... not yet anyway. "They've told us not to wear our 'Nam bracelets, so I keep mine under wraps." I lifted my arm and tugged my sleeve. "I want out of the army, and away from here. And the sooner, the better." At that point, I considered my bracelet an extension of me, no longer an article of clothing.

"Cool. Hey, I got killer weed. Want to smoke?" Brett asked.

"Yeah, after I ditch these duds."

The smell of burnt Mary J welcomed me through Brett's door, and I picked up with him where I'd left off with Wayne, Jim, and Curt.

* * *

247

Several days later, I lay on my couch in my skivvies, soaking up cooled air as I reread the letter I'd received that day from Pam. I concentrated on part of one sentence:

… moved into an apartment and met three nice guys in the building.

Met other guys? Three?

A read between the words didn't settle the issue. Instead, my imagination added fuel. What did she mean? I imagined her hanging out in their apartment and attending their parties. Imagined she hinted at wanting a serious relationship with them … or any male other than me.

Pam and I had never disagreed. We had always been easy and gentle toward each other. Was she giving me the brush-off? Whispering goodbye? Had she been disappointed over our sex together, too?

Knock, knock, knock!

"Hey, the pusher man just pulled in," Brett said, somewhat out of breath. "Stopped off on his way north. He's got hash, grass, acid, and speed." He'd rattled that off like a kid taking inventory in a candy store. "Come on over to my place."

How well does Brett know that guy? Had that guy been tailed? Was he under surveillance? I needed a break from Pam's letter, so I set my reservations aside. With caution in the shit-can, I headed over to check out the goods. A voice from the back of my mind warned me to avoid the drug abyss and keep myself in check. *Maybe I'll just maneuver along the recreational edges.*

After an examination of the dealer's supply, I copped a few tabs of acid and a baggie of weed. I didn't want to hold a big stash and face a life-wrecking bust. I figured jail would be worse than my army life.

* * *

I enjoyed Brett's company, but when his summer active duty ended, he headed home to Tennessee. Another friend lost, but my spin on it? That loss was for the best. Brett was tempting a serious drug bust and I didn't want to end up in the slammer next to him.

Pam's words remained stuck in my head, and with no other letters to contradict my suspicion, it seemed to me she'd written me a gentle Dear John.

I didn't respond to her letter. Should've but didn't. I didn't want to say goodbye to her and didn't want to see her hurt, nor did I want to face the finality of a goodbye from her. I opted for silence—the coward's way out, easier for me than a kick-upside-the-head rejection with the question, What part of "Dear John" did you not understand?

Yet, my questions wouldn't go away. Had she really been breaking up with me? Or was it me who'd done so by not sending her any more letters? Regardless, I never heard from her again.

WILD MAN

Me? Cold, bare, shriveled, and dormant, waiting in hope of the coming spring, not that different from the Kentucky winter landscape. I'd started adjustment to civilian life with little idea what that would be, beyond the fact that no military-uniformed jerks lurked in the background to dictate my every move. College lay in the future, a place to get on with my life. My prison sentence in green fatigues had ended with a three-month-twenty-something-day early release for seasonal employment. I'd bid Fort Bragg good riddance about three months earlier, and considered that a jailbreak. Marking time until WKU's winter semester started, I helped Dad with his carpentry and construction work.

I'd been spending a good portion of my weekends drinking and hanging around Verlon's apartment. At that point, he'd moved from home and shared a place with two friends. I'd given another of Verlon's friends a ride over earlier that Saturday evening, but hours later he asked me for a ride home. I hadn't wanted to do that, but reluctantly agreed, though I felt tired and pissed.

Driving in the half-frozen air of late night, belly full of booze, it all welled up. I was sick and tired of feeling put upon for my free taxi service. *Mooch.*

I jammed my foot to the floorboard, and my three-eighty-three cubic-inch Road Runner engine roared to life and accelerated us down the deserted street—one I'd driven many times. At the bottom of the railroad overpass, one sign read, BRIDGES FREEZE BEFORE ROADWAY, and a bold black arrow on another indicated a left bend beyond the rise. No surprise to me.

Everything went well enough until I crested the ice-covered bridge, where I lost control and the street began its left turn.

BAM! The curb on the right side didn't stop me.

BAM! The guardrail on the right side redirected me to the left as metal scraped against metal, my car versus the railing.

I applied the brakes full-on. Tires screeched on the dry pavement beyond the bridge as we skidded down the overpass.

No other vehicles were in sight. At least I had that going in my favor.

The traffic signal, where the street straightened at the bottom of the hill, changed from green to yellow. I knew I had little choice where I'd come to a stop; however, I pulled the steering wheel hard to the right in hopes of avoiding entering the intersection or hitting the center median.

Sideways.

I couldn't react fast enough to regain control.

CRASH!!!

The silence seemed deafening, though neighborhood dogs soon began barking in the distance. I realized I sat broadside against a utility pole. The dashboard and hood were crumpled at odd angles. The windshield was shattered. The front edge of my door hugged the telephone pole within arm's reach.

My wide-eyed passenger grabbed his door handle and pulled. "I'll walk home," he said.

Yeah. Go ahead. Run.

Didn't take him long to disappear, as I sat alone at the scene. *Any pain? No. Run? That won't work.* I tossed my car keys out of the window. *Where the hell had that idea come from?* I didn't see myself prone to irrational ideas in general, but that one took the cake.

After the fact, desperate, I rationalized that action as my best option available. And I hit upon telling the cops that since I couldn't drive, I wouldn't be a menace to anyone if they let me walk—flimsy though that argument was.

And my anger? I knew where that had come from … at least thought I knew. Pretty sure I knew, anyway, but I sat shocked by its sudden intensity, a replay of that call-girl scene in Osaka. I knew I'd fucked up big-time, and perhaps I was more like Dad than I cared to admit. "Sober up. Get control of yourself," I mumbled and swore, "No more taxi service."

Within several minutes a squad car pulled up, red and blue lights flashing. Two cops emerged.

One officer held a flashlight on my face from the passenger side. The other questioned me through the driver's side. "This your car?" that one said. "You got a license and registration?"

I pulled out the necessary paperwork and passed it to him.

The officer by the passenger door directed me to get out, then ushered me to the backseat of their patrol car.

Facing jail time? Headed for the drunk tank?

That same officer continued his interrogation. "What happened?"

"I hit a patch of ice on the bridge," I said, which was true, I believed.

At that point the other officer had joined us in their vehicle. "What's the speed limit here?" he asked.

I figured I'd topped sixty, at least, when I'd lost control, but to play that off I padded my guess. "Thirty-five, I think."

"No, twenty-five," he said.

Busted! Surrender my best course of action? "Well, you got me, then," I said.

He wrote a note—I couldn't see what—and showed the other cop, who nodded.

My gut knotted. *Jail for sure!*

They passed a note or two to each other, and conferred in code, while we waited for an all-clear about the status of my driver's license and vehicle registration. When it came, one of them asked me, "You got a way to get home?"

Huh? "My brother's place isn't that far. I can walk there." I didn't dare say another word.

"Okay. You can go," one cop said.

Without hesitation I got out of their squad car. I didn't want to give them the impression of desperation, despite feeling that way.

By the time I'd walked back to Verlon's apartment, I'd sobered.

* * *

The next day, the scene didn't appear any prettier to me. In fact, in broad daylight, with a clearer head and an opportunity to examine the full extent of damage, I considered myself lucky to have escaped injury … or worse. Even at a glance, anyone could see that I'd turned my Road Runner into a scrap heap, beyond totaled.

Dad helped me tow my mangled assemblage of metal, rubber, and glass home. I expected a lecture from him, though one never came.

To avoid being sued or jailed, I paid the utility company for a new pole without hesitation when they sent me a bill. Then, I sold my Road Runner to a wrecking yard—more like unloaded it onto them—and replaced it with a cheap set of wheels.

* * *

My sociology classes at Western Kentucky University started several weeks later. I felt free to focus on learning for its own sake—not for any job, and not for the pursuit of money. As well, I planned to take full advantage of my GI Bill benefits, since I'd left the army with an honorable discharge.

I attended classes for several semesters, then moved to a different apartment. The total darkness and near silence in Bogle Hall, an off-campus '60s-era concrete-block bomb shelter converted to an apartment complex, provided me with a sanctuary cubbyhole.

I joined VOC, Veterans On Campus, a mature version of the silly-ass fraternities. No rush week or hazing required. I accepted, as I figured they did also, that we'd pledged in 'Nam as FNGs, newbies, and cherries. I understood we'd experienced life and American culture through the lens of 'Nam. Knew we hadn't just read about 'Nam or watched it on TV. We'd lived 'Nam. We'd smelled 'Nam. We'd seen and heard 'Nam, eaten 'Nam, slept 'Nam. Collectively, we'd looked into the eyes of its people, and though there to better their lives, we'd killed many of them.

A few of the VOC members remained clean-cut, studied business and economics, and wore sports coats with ties as if they hadn't been affected by Vietnam in any way. Others acted peculiar or seemed numb. Didn't take me long to learn which ones used drugs, because I did, too. I related to them, and they accepted me.

At VOC socials I encountered receptive college girls. Couldn't believe my luck. But I worked to present myself in the best light and as a suitable sexual prospect. I kept my flaws hidden: my anger; cynicism about American purity of purpose and moral superiority; that suicidal episode in Japan; my herpes; my car crash; anything and everything I figured that would be a sexual turnoff to a potential partner.

But nothing prevented my recurring dream.

In fatigues on a dusty, desolate base I'm wandering in the pitch-black of night.

I'm in the army again. How the hell did that happen? One stint in the army, and with an honorable discharge to prove it, I'll search for someone to hear my story, correct the injustice done me, and get out. I'll talk to the CO or at least a clerk at the unit headquarters.

I find a building, lit from within, where several guys are talking and laughing.

Has to be the headquarters office, where I can plead my case.

The door's locked, and try as I might, they pay no attention to me.

Don't see me? Don't hear me?

My dreams were surely nothing as bad as Dad's nightmares after WWII, but they were my drafted-and-shipped-to-'Nam version, regardless. Likely, they were triggered by the seven years of my "reserve" status following discharge, which subjected me to a recall to active duty at the President's say?

I hadn't realized "reserve" status to be part of the deal at my draft induction or subsequent enlistment. No one had mentioned that fact, an omission that hit me like an outright lie. And I'd only learned about it when I examined my DD-214 at discharge. What a slap upside the head! I thought my discharge was to be a jailbreak, but it turned out to be more like a parole, with me still under "the man's" thumb.

I wondered if I'd ever be free of the army.

* * *

With good grades and steady progress toward a B.A. in sociology and a minor in social work, and with a set of wheels and steady sex with a willing woman for whom I had real feelings, I'd considered myself on the right track. Everything had seemed under control despite my bad dreams … until a steady sex partner gave me the brush-off. That "breaking news" flattened me, and she didn't give me a reason. I thought I loved her. I thought about her all the time.

In the med center for the third or fourth time—I'd lost track—to get relief for a recurring gut-ache, I knew something had to give.

"I can give you atropine," the university medical center doctor said. "I'll need to go get my script pad." He rose from his stool and left the exam room.

Jesus. They'd told us in Basic that atropine was a poison and trained us how to use it as an antidote for nerve gas. *And the doc doesn't have his script pad? What the hell is that guy up to?*

Alone in the dark and quiet of my refuge with my bit of girlfriend rejection, Bogle Hall had turned on me and threatened to become my tomb when suicidal thoughts offered me escape from my turmoil. But I still clung to the notion of a future. After all, I'd survived Vietnam and the army. I'd need to fight to survive, not by battling Charlie or the army, but by battling a self-destructive part of myself. I knew, though, that I wouldn't survive those thoughts and feelings all on my own.

The young doc, not much older than me, returned. Before he took his seat, I blurted, "I don't want to be this way anymore." On the verge of sobbing, tears welled in my eyes.

"What's going on?" the doc asked kindly.

I confessed about being isolated. Admitted my shit wasn't together, and that I had suicidal thoughts.

He remained calm and with a measured voice, said, "Are you willing to see a counselor?"

My breath lost, like from an unseen gut punch, the word gushed past my quivering lips. "Yes." *There. I've opened the door. Bared my gaping wound. Perhaps I won't succumb to my inner turmoil like Jellybean or Uncle Tunney.*

I'd worked hard to keep everything together since day one in the army—to appear adequate, to avoid a loss of control, and not get busted for fighting, although I'd come close more times than I cared to remember. Now, however, no longer wearing dog tags and puke-green fatigues, I resembled my crumpled heap of Road-Runner scrap metal, both inside and out. And I'd never admitted to anyone, not a single soul, that my shit wasn't together—until there, at the med center.

The doc's voice remained steady and confident. "I know a good counselor and I think she can help you." He picked up the phone receiver nearby and dialed the university counseling center. "I want to schedule an appointment," he told somebody on the other end of the line. He looked at me. "Next Tuesday morning okay?"

A long way off. I hoped I could make it. I nodded and accepted the appointment card the way a drowning man grabs a lifeline. "Thank you." Tears wet my face.

I wanted to hide from the horrified look on the young female receptionist's face whom I saw out of the corner of my eye as I hurried to the med center exit. I figured the doc had spilled the beans and she could see my darkest secrets.

* * *

Monday, one more day until my appointment, I crossed paths with another VOC member in the student center.

"Hey, wild man, what's up?" he asked.

It was hard for me to read his usual flip manner and deadpan stare, which made me uneasy. *Wired wrong? What had he done in 'Nam?* I visualized him pulling a knife in the shadows and stabbing away, while I recognized his reference to my honky's scraggly version of an Afro and untrimmed mountain-man beard. *God, what have I become?* I didn't want to go near the subject of my misery with him. *Antagonize him and end up his next victim?*

"I don't have time to talk," I said. "I'm headed to class." Looking back, I realize I didn't know what he'd experienced in 'Nam, had no way of knowing his deepest thoughts and feelings, and that I'd projected my ideas onto him.

I railed as I walked away from him and thought, *Don't judge me, damn you.* I railed against everyone whom I thought judged me, frustrated about changing how and what they thought about me, based on my appearance: my long hair and beard, my clothes. Who knew what? My ideas, my smell, my cheap wheels? How dare they? They didn't understand me or what I'd seen. *See me, an individual.*

But I judged other people. I'd learned to appreciate everyday American things while in Vietnam and saw what I considered the petty day-to-day concerns of younger students around me, most fresh out of high school. They were ignorant and shallow and had no clue about Vietnam or the gift given them by the virtue of their birth.

* * *

On Tuesday, I sat across from my therapist, Ms. Alpee, and peering out from behind my barbwire-topped fence, opened up my festered wounds.

Over the next months, I talked with Ms. Alpee about my feelings and issues, something I had never dared to do before. I brought copies of books by leading authors in the fields of psychology, sociology, and philosophy that I was studying at the time, such as Eric Fromm's *Man for Himself,* to our sessions. Citing passages that I'd underlined or the questions I'd written in the margins, we explored my understanding of feelings, attitudes, and ideas.

Ms. Alpee became my psychological anchor and I attended my sessions faithfully. On the occasions when she canceled a session, informing me of her need to attend to another student's crisis, I felt adrift. And though jealous of the other student and hating to miss those sessions, I accepted my losses without protest, trusting that their situations were more desperate than mine at those moments.

My suicidal feelings and thoughts gradually abated, for which I was grateful. I concluded my sessions with Ms. Alpee a few months before I graduated from WKU. At that point, I felt on solid ground, and though my life wasn't perfect, I could see a future.

AFTERWORD

Following my graduation from WKU, I immigrated to California where I earned a MA in Marriage, Family, and Child Counseling, then worked in the field of alcohol/drug rehabilitation. And over a number of years, while assisting others in their recovery processes, I had opportunity to gain a healthier perspective on emotional expression through catharsis.

While in the army and Vietnam, I'd stumbled my way toward manhood while exploring the use of alcohol, drugs, sex, and anger in an attempt to survive a year in a strange world where I never wanted to be. And additionally, trauma having many faces, I'd struggled to deal with the path on which mine took me.

All of our Vietnam service personnel, both men and women— for that matter, all veterans everywhere and whenever—suffered trauma, I believe. No doubt some have overcome the worst of their issues, though some have not. And then there are those who have succumbed to theirs. Though exact figures of Vietnam vet suicides are not available, all U.S. veteran suicides averaged 6,000 per year over the ten-year span of 2008 to 2017. That's 60,000!

I want to say to all our veterans: Welcome home. And to everyone struggling with their version of trauma, regardless of its source: You don't need to face your demons alone.